SMART

English Grammar and Composition

Workbook and References for aspirants of Continuing Education

Chandan Sengupta

Creative Learning Series

SMART English Grammar and Composition

Edited by Chandan Sengupta

Published by   : Chandan Sengupta

ISBN   : **9798887837086**

Year of Publication   : 2024

Date of Publication   : 05/08/2024

Place of Publication   : Arabinda Nagar Bankura , 722101 (WB)

In a wider perspective this workbook can be used as a reference material by other fellows. The Question Bank addresses patterns of problems of all possible levels. So there is no specific boundary of distinction of any class or any specific stream of study. Any aspirant remaining engaged in regular studies can have access to this Question Bank. Materials used here were collected from various sources and are also cross checked for finding out specific difficulties. We effectively sortlisted such areas and prepared a revised edition of this volume. This question bank module can also be a helpful companion for aspirants who seek admission in different strams of jobs, services and fellowships for which they have to opt for some examinations duly conducted by UPSC, PSC, SSC, RRB or any other boards of study. This workbook will provide an ample scope to students of high School standard to improve skills related to language and inter—personal communication. Communication process in modern world should be digitally sound also. We aspire for higher scope of progress as students involving in active communication process gains a lot.

Font size of some of the practice papers are kept small for ensuring accommodation of the material of large volume. Students of higher class can explore them with an ease. They may not feel any specific problem while moving through content areas.

This book is dedicated to fellow aspirants of Continuing Education.

Contents

Foreword

There is no end if we start incorporating different aspects related to English Grammar along with expanded exercises. Job seekers require some sort of practice materials as per the prescribed formats issued to them by board of examiners. We also consider some additional practice materials for gaining mastery upon concepts and perspectives of the rules related to writing and speaking a language. This publication is prepared accordingly to address ever growing need of fellow students of the higher levels of studies. Students of other faculties can also opt for this publication with an apprehension of gaining advancement in the allied fields of studies. There are reference materials in plenty.[1] Some of such materials are of higher importance and some are at the basic stage. Our aspirants require some practice materials which fits better with the context. Best use of the language is another aspect depending upon which we select language related practice materials.

It is also recommended that aspirants should prepare daily routine for practicing best uses of grammar and vocabulary on the basis of materials provided to them. Some of the materials obtained from old scriptures and great writings. We also worked out some self - learning modules along with suggested solutions to equip the fellow learner with background materials needed for accelerating self-study. These materials will punctuate the use of language in relation to the modern context. We also propose that students should maintain an expanded list of vocabularies so that timely need of the same can be fulfilled. It will also enhance the learning skills of the fellow student by providing them some better alternatives to be used.

One should keep in mind that language is considered as a personality booster. We learn English Grammar for gaining mastery in speaking and writing English perfectly. We also learn different rules of writing for confirming our skill of writing and speaking in the context of the modern communication system. It is also becoming evident from our systematic studies that we use only a part of speaking and writing alternatives to express our views and concerns on some of the parts of our .communication formats.

This Workbook is prepared for providing supporting content and comprehensive guidance to aspirants of different examinations, such as UPSC, PSC, SSC, RRB, Bank Probationary Officer's Examination and other competitive examinations conducted by different boards of studies. Basic framework of the syllabus is taken up from the content areas prescribed by Central Board of Secondary Educations for English Communicative Programmes. It will be equally helpful for teachers and other associates having passion of providing quality guidance along with time tested practice materials.

Equal strength is provided on both grammar rules and communication skills. Some of the fundamentals are duly incorporated to make the content area a balanced one for the fellow aspirants. Incorporation of some of the basic templates is avoided for keeping the volume of this workbook in limit. One can take support of any of the grammar and comprehension handbook for gaining mastery in all such basic formats. This workbook will imply focus on the higher levels of English Grammar and Compositions.

---

[1] *Meiklejohn's "English Language," Longmans' "School Grammar," West's "English Grammar," Bain's "Higher English Grammar" and "Composition Grammar," Sweet's "Primer of Spoken English" and "New English Grammar," etc., Hodgson's "Errors in the Use of English," Morris's "Elementary Lessons in Historical English Grammar," Lounsbury's "English Language," Champney's "History of English," Emerson's "History of the English Language," Kellner's "Historical Outlines of English Syntax," Earle's "English Prose," and Matzner's "Englische Grammatik." Allen's "Subjunctive Mood in English," Battler's articles on "Prepositions" in the "Anglia,"*

Improve Your Vocabulary

Prefixes and Suffixes :
Pre means before, fix means set. Adding prefix before a word we can create new word.
For Eg: able- enable; understand – misunderstand; belief- disbelief; etc…

Suffixes are used after a word to create new words.
For Eg: Teach- Teacher; Agree- Agreement; etc…

In fact, if you study the shape of a word, you can divide into three parts- the prefix, suffix, and the root word.
Let us now study some prefixes and suffixes and see the words that can be formed by using them:

Some of the tips to learn Vocabulary;
The prefix 'RE 'means back or again.
For Eg:
rebuild -------RE build means Build again
recall------ RE call means to bring back to mind or remember.
Refold ------ RE fold means fold again.
Regain ----- RE gain means get back.
Remind ------ RE mind means mention again
Repay ------ RE pay means payback.
--- You try to write some more like this…..

The root PORT means carry
For Eg:
Port ---- PORT means a place ships may wait in.
Porter ------ PORT er means one who carries things, as baggage.
Deport ----- de PORT means to send a person away.
Report ------- re PORT means an account of something which happened.
Support ---- sup PORT means to carry along with help.
Portable --- PORT able means can be carried.
----- practice some more like this…..

The prefixes EN and EM means into/ in
For Eg:
endanger ---- EN danger means put into danger
Enroll ----- EN roll means to enter or register.
Entrust ----- EN trust means charge with a specified office or duty involving trust.
Enslave ---- EN slave means put into slavery.
Embrace ------ EM brace means to take into one's arms.

Embark ------- EM bark means get into a train or ship a for journey.

The suffix ATE means to cause or make.
For Eg:
dedicate ----- dedic ATE means to set apart for a purpose.
Advocate ----- advoc ATE means to speak for to defend.
Deviate ---- Devi ATE means to turn aside from the right way.
Liquidate ----- liquid ATE means to end a debt by payment.
educate ----- educ ATE means to lead to knowledge.
enumarate ----- enumar ATE means to count.

The Root MEM means REMEMBER.
For Eg:
memento ----- MEM ento means something to make one remember.
Memorandum ---- MEM orandum means a reminder.
Memory ------ MEM ory means the ability to recall.
Memoir ------ MEM oir means a record of a thing to remember.
Memorable ------- MEM orable means worth remembering.
In memoriam ------ In MEM oriam means In memory of.

The root UNI means ONE.
For Eg:
Unique ----- UNI que means one of a kind.
Union ---- UNI on means the joining of many into one.
Unitarianism ----- UNI tarianism means a belief in one god.
Unanimous ----- UN animous means having one opinion held by all.
Universe ----- UNI verse means all parts of the world as one.
Unimanual ---- UNI manual means done with one hand.
So, such these root words offer you an easy step – by-step approach to an understanding of thousands of words in the English Language.

Examples
The new pattern vocabulary is nothing but an Analogy. It means comparison, relation, resemblance and correlation. The Analogy s are given in exams to test the analytical ability of yours.
You will find word analogies, or verbal analogies, used in standardized tests and sometimes in job interviews where you must show the relationship between two objects or

concepts using logic and reasoning. These analogies are set up in a standard format. For Eg: tree: leaf:: flower: petal. An analogy is more of a logical argument than a simple figure of speech.

Now I will explain to you the basic level of analogy s.

Read all the choices before choosing your answer.

Finding out a right choice from given options reveal your smartness in thinking.

In the following s, you are required to identify and assess the logical relationship between a given pair of words in the , then choose a pair of words from the options that exhibit the same logical relationship as the original pair in the s.

1. Grove: Forest : --------- : Lake.
a. pond
b .ocean
c. tree
d. boat.
Ans: a. Pond,
Explanation: A grove is a similar version of a forest, and a pond is a smaller version of a lake.

2. Spelunker: -------- : : Astronomer : Space
a. spaceship   b. light   c. cave   d. wave
Ans: c. cave
Explanation: A spelunker is someone explores caves, and an astronomer is someone who explores space.

3. Mend: Sewing:: Edit : ---------
a. darn   b. repair   c. manuscript   d. makeshift
Ans: c.Manuscript.
Explanation: one fixes sewing by mending; one fixes manuscript by editing.

4. Perfidy: -------- : : satire : Parody
a. treachery   b. humour   c. forgiveness   d. performance.
Ans: a. treachery
Explanation: Perfidy is synonym for treachery, and satire is a synonym for parody.

5. Hawali: 1959:: ------- 1912
a. Network   b. South Carolina   c. Arizona   d. Maine
Ans: c.Arizona
Explanation: Hawaii became a state in 1959, and Arizona became a state in 1912.

6. Rotation: Earth:: -------- : Top
a. planet   b. spinning   c. sun   d. expanding
Ans: Spinning
Explanation: Rotation is the movement of the earth and spinning is the movement of a top.

7. Piercing: ------ : : Hushed : Whisper
a. diamond   b. watch   c. siren   d. ears
Ans: Siren
Explanation: A siren is described as piercing, and a whisper is described as hushed.

8. Cabal: -------- : : Output : Yield.
a. Plot
b.plant
c. cable
d. stop.
Ans: a. Plot
Explanation: Cabal is a synonym for plot, and Output is a synonym for Yield.

9. Channel: Waterway :: -------- : Fabric
a. polyester   b. zipper   c. cotton   d. stone
Ans: c. Cotton
Explanation: A channel is a natural water way, and cotton is a natural fabric.

10. Penurious: -------- : : Deep : Significant
a. generous   b.stingy   c. decrepit   d. cavernous
Ans: b.stingy
Explanation: Penurious is a synonym for stingy, and deep is a synonym for significant

11. ------- : Flood :: Helmet: Injury
a. drowned   b.Coast Guard   c.river   d.levee
Ans : d. levee
Explanation: A levee prevents a flood, and a helmet prevents injury.

12. Rein : Horse :: Control panel : ------
a. Pilot   b. bit   c. plane   d. rider
Ans: plane
Explanation: A rider uses a rein to guide a horse; a pilot uses the control panel to guide a plane.

13. Spoke : : -------- Word : Sentence
a. speaker   b. paragraph   c. comma   d. wheel
Ans: d.wheel.
Explanation: A spoke is part of a wheel, and a word is part of a sentence.

14. Confederate: -------- : : Narrator: Chronicler
a. north   b. partner   c. history   d. teacher.
Ans: b.partner
Explanation: A confederate is a synonym for a partner, and a narrator is a synonym for chronicler.

15. Search : --------- :: Defeat : Vanquish
a. Peer   b. ransack   c. destroy   d. find
Ans: b. ransack
Explanation: To ransack is to search thoroughly, and to vanquish is defeat thoroughly.

16. Dolorous: ------ : : Sonorous : Loud
a. woozy   b. weepy   c. dull   d. sleepy
Ans: weepy
Explanation: Dolorous is a synonym for weepy, and Sonorous is a synonym for loud.

17. Knave: ------- : : Coward : Bravery
a. retreat.   b.beauty   c.truth   d. stoicism
Ans: c. truth
Explanation: A knave is one who does not exhibits the truth, and a coward does not exhibit bravery.

18. Cushion: Sofa : : Shelf: --------
a. Ledge   b. bookcase   c. storage   d. frame
Ans: b. bookcase
Explanation: A cushion is a part of a sofa, and a shelf is a part of a bookcase.

19. Enfeeble: Forty :: Concede : ----------
a. dispute   b.close   c.expect   d.surrender
Ans: a. dispute
Explanation: To enfeeble is an antonym of to fortify, and to concede is an antonym of to dispute.

20. Secret: Furtive :: Audible : ------
a. resonant   b.nap   c. sack   d.ring
Ans: a. resonant
Explanation: Furtive is more intensely secret, and resonant is more intensely audible.

21. Thresher : ------- :: Mastiff : Dog
a. robin   b. master   c. shark   d.policeman
Ans: c.shark
Explanation: Thresher is a type of shark, and Mastiff is a type of dog.

Important

Important English Vocabulary

1). Amenity (Noun)
Definition: A desirable or useful feature or facility of a building or place.
Synonyms: Facility, service, convenience, resource, utility
Usage: the property is situated in a convenient location, close to all local amenities.

2). Fret (Verb)
Definition: be constantly or visibly anxious.
Synonyms: worry, be anxious, feel uneasy, be distressed
Usage: the workers fretted about being displaced by machines

3). Notion (Noun)
Definition: a conception of or belief about something.
Synonyms: idea, belief, concept, conception, conviction, opinion,
Usage: children have different notions about the roles of their parents

4). Absurd (Adj)
Definition: wildly unreasonable, illogical, or inappropriate.
Synonyms: preposterous, ridiculous, ludicrous, farcical, laughable
Usage: the allegations are patently absurd.

5). Thickets (Noun)
Definition: a dense group of bushes or trees.
Synonyms: copse, dense growth, grove, brake, clump
Usage: a horned owl perfectly camouflaged in a dense thicket.

6). Reliant (Adj)
Definition: dependent on someone or something.
Synonyms: relying, relative, depending, controlled by
Usage: the company is heavily reliant on the baby market.

7). Coalition (Noun)
Definition: a temporary alliance for combined action, especially of political parties forming a government.
Synonyms: alliance, union, partnership, affiliation
Usage: the general election saw no change in the ruling four-party coalition.

8). Dire (Adj)
Definition: extremely serious or urgent.
Synonyms: Terrible, dreadful, frightful, awful, horrible
Usage: misuse of drugs can have dire consequences.

9). Audited (Verb)
Definition: conduct an official financial inspection of (a company or its accounts).
Synonyms: Inspect, examine, survey, look over, go over
Usage: unlimited companies must also have their accounts audited.

10). Reckons (Verb)
Definition: be of the opinion.
Synonyms: believe, think, be of the opinion, be of the view
Usage: he reckons that the army should pull out entirely.

11). Elusive (Adj)
Definition: difficult to find, catch, or achieve.
Synonyms: slippery, informal always on the move
Usage: He tried to reach her by telephone, but she continued to be elusive.

12). Dispute (Verb)
Definition: argue about (something).
Synonyms: debate, discuss, clash
Usage: George visited him and disputed with him.

13). Dichotomy (Noun)
Definition: a division or contrast between two things that are or are represented as being opposed or entirely different.
Synonyms: division, separation, split
Usage: There is a great dichotomy between social theory and practice.

14). Stipulation (Noun)
Definition: a condition or requirement that is specified or demanded as part of an agreement.
Synonyms: condition, provision, specification
Usage: They donated their collection of prints with the stipulation that they never be publicly exhibited.

15). Alleviate (Verb)
Definition: make (suffering, deficiency, or a problem) less severe.
Synonyms: reduce, ease, relieve, diminish, lessen
Usage: He couldn't prevent her pain, only alleviate it.

16). Lurk (Verb)
Definition: be or remain hidden so as to wait in ambush for someone or something.
Synonyms: hide, steal, take cover
Usage: A ruthless killer still lurked in the darkness.

17). Divergent (Adj)
Definition: tending to be different or develop in different directions.
Synonyms: differing, varying, dissimilar, unlike
Usage: They adopted divergent approaches to almost every issue.

18). Amass (Verb)
Definition: gather together or accumulate (a large amount or number of material or things) over a period of time.
Synonyms: gather, collect, assemble, accumulate

Usage: He amassed a fortune estimated at close to a million pounds.

19). Consensus (Noun)
Definition: a general agreement
Synonyms: agreement, harmony, concord
Usage: There is a growing consensus that the current regime has failed.

20). Veto (Verb)
Definition: exercise a veto against (a decision or proposal).
Synonyms: reject, dismiss, block
Usage: The president carried out his threat to veto the bill.

21). Wrangle (Verb)
Definition: have a long, complicated dispute or argument.
Synonyms: argue, quarrel, debate
Usage: Negotiators had wrangled over details of the agreement.

22). Contingency (Noun)
Definition: a future event or circumstance which is possible but cannot be predicted with certainty.
Synonyms: eventuality, incident, happening, occurrence
Usage: A detailed contract which attempts to provide for all possible contingencies.

23). Avert (Verb)
Definition: turn away (one's eyes or thoughts).
Synonyms: turn aside, turn away, turn to one side
Usage: She averted her eyes while we made stilted conversation.

24). Schism (Noun)
Definition: a split or division between strongly opposed sections or parties, caused by differences in opinion or belief.
Synonyms: division, split, separation
Usage: The widening schism between church leaders and politicians.

25). Inevitable (Adj)
Definition: certain to happen; unavoidable.
Synonyms: unavoidable, inescapable, unpreventable
Usage: His resignation was inevitable.

26). Robust (Adj)
Definition: strong and healthy; vigorous.
Synonyms: strong, vigorous, sturdy, tough
Usage: The Caplan family are a robust lot.

27). Fork (Verb)
Definition: (especially of a route) divide into two parts.
Synonyms: branch, split, divide, separate
Usage: The place where the road forks.

28). Sober (Adj)
Definition: serious, sensible, and solemn.
Synonyms: thoughtful, grave, sombre, severe, earnest
Usage: A sober view of life.

29). Unveil (Verb)
Definition: show or announce publicly for the first time.
Synonyms: disclose, make known, reveal
Usage: The club has unveiled plans for a new 1600-seat stand.

30). Rig (Verb)
Definition: set up (equipment or a device or structure), typically in a makeshift or hasty way.
Synonyms: set up hastily, erect hastily, assemble hastily, throw together
Usage: He had rigged up a sort of tent.

31). Entrench (Verb)
Definition: establish (an attitude, habit, or belief) so firmly that change is very difficult or unlikely.
Synonyms: establish, settle, ensconce, lodge, set
Usage: This country is entrenched in a litigation mentality.

32). Ebbs (Verb)
Definition: (of tidewater) move away from the land; recede.
Synonyms: recede, go out, retreat, flow back
Usage: The tide ebbed in the afternoon.

33). Dearth (Noun)
Definition: a scarcity or lack of something.
Synonyms: lack, scarcity, shortfall, scarceness
Usage: There is a dearth of properly trained specialists.

34). Lure (Verb)
Definition: tempt (a person or animal) to do something or to go somewhere, especially by offering some form of reward.
Synonyms: tempt, entice, attract, induce.
Usage: Consumers are frequently lured into debt by clever advertising.

35). Pursuit (Noun)
Definition: the action of pursuing someone or something.
Synonyms: chasing, pursuing, stalking, tracking
Usage: The organization is devoted to the pursuit of profit.

36). Substantially (Adveb)
Definition: to a great or significant extent.
Synonyms: considerably, significantly, greatly, a great deal
Usage: The cost of oil imports has fallen substantially.

37). Laggards (Noun)

Definition: a person who makes slow progress and falls behind others.
Synonyms: straggler, loiterer, lingerer, dawdler, sluggard, slug, snail
Usage: Staff were under enormous pressure and there was no time for laggards.

38). Wither (Verb)
Definition: fall into decay or decline.
Synonyms: diminish, dwindle, lessen, fade
Usage: It is not true that old myths either die or wither away.

39). Surge (Verb)
Definition: (of a crowd or a natural force) move suddenly and powerfully forward or upward.
Synonyms: gush, rush, flow

40). Amid (Preposition)
Definition: surrounded by; in the middle of.
Synonyms: in the middle of, among, between
Usage: Our dream home, set amid magnificent rolling countryside.

41). Spur (Noun)
Definition: a thing that prompts or encourages someone; an incentive.
Synonyms: Stimulus, incentive, encourangement
Usage: The outcome of the election added a further spur to the reform movement.

42). Jolt (Verb)
Definition: push or shake (someone or something) abruptly and roughly.
Synonyms: push, bump, shake
Usage: The train stopped suddenly, jolting the passengers to one side.

43). Chime (Verb)
Definition: be in agreement with.
Synonyms: accord, correspond, agree
Usage: His poem chimes with our modern experience of loss.

44). Lucrative (Adj)
Definition: producing a great deal of profit.
Synonyms: Profitable, gainful, remunerative, moneymaking
Usage: A lucrative career as a stand-up comedian.

45). Constraints (Noun)
Definition: a limitation or restriction.
Synonyms: impediment, obstruction, restraint
Usage: The availability of water is the main constraint on food production.

46). Ethnic (Adj)
Definition: relating to a population subgroup (within a larger or dominant national or cultural group) with a common national or cultural tradition.
Synonyms: racial, race-related, ethnological, genetic
Usage: Ethnic and cultural rights and traditions.

47). Pogroms (Noun)
Definition: an organized massacre of a particular ethnic group, in particular that of Jews in Russia or eastern Europe.
Synonyms: massacre, slaughter, wholesale slaughter, mass slaughter, mass killing
Usage: The Nazis began a pogrom against Jewish people in Germany.

48). Contemporary (Adj)
Definition: belonging to or occurring in the present.
Synonyms: modern, present-day, present, current, present-time, immediate
Usage: The tension and complexities of our contemporary society.

49). Rely (Verb)
Definition: depend on with full trust or confidence.
Synonyms: count, bank, place reliance, bargain, plan
Usage: I know I can rely on your discretion.

50). Instance (Noun)
Definition: an example or single occurrence of something.
Synonyms: example, occasion, occurrence, case, representative case
Usage: There was not a single instance of religious persecution.

51). Expulsion (Noun)
Definition: the action of forcing someone to leave an organization.
Synonyms: removal, debarment, dismissal, exclusion, discharge
Usage: They faced expulsion from the party.

52). Scapegoats (Noun)
Definition: a person who is blamed for the wrongdoings, mistakes, or faults of others, especially for reasons of expediency.
Synonyms: whipping boy, victim
Usage: The older boy bullied his younger brother into being the scapegoat for the crime he committed.

53). Discernible (Adj)
Definition: able to be discerned; perceptible.
Synonyms: visible, detectable, noticeable, perceptible, observable
Usage: The figure was scarcely discernible in the pale moonlight.

54). Soothe (Verb)
Definition: gently calm (a person or their feelings).
Synonyms: calm, calm down, quiet, pacify

Usage: A shot of brandy might soothe his nerves.
55). Boon (Noun)
Definition: a thing that is helpful or beneficial.
Synonyms: blessing, godsend, bonus, good thing, benefit
Usage: The route will be a boon to many travellers.
56). Acquire (Verb)
Definition: buy or obtain (an asset or object) for oneself.
Synonyms: obtain, come by, come to have, get, receive, gain
Usage: She acquired a collection of fine art prints
57). Intentions (Noun)
Definition: a thing intended; an aim or plan.
Synonyms: aim, purpose, objective, goal
Usage: She was full of good intentions.
58). Presumably (Adverb)
Definition: used to convey that what is asserted is very likely though not known for certain.
Synonyms: I assume, I expect, I believe, I presume, I take it, I suppose
Usage: It was not yet ten o'clock, so presumably the boys were still at the pub.
59). Punt (Verb)
Definition: travel or convey in a punt.
Usage: In summer you can enjoy punting along the river.
60). Ironically (Adverb)
Definition: used in reference to a paradoxical, unexpected, or coincidental situation.
Usage: ironically, the rescue craft which saved her was the boat she was helping to pay for.
61). Splurged (Verb)
Definition: spend (money) freely or extravagantly
Usage: I'd splurged about Rs. 2,500 on clothes.
62). Expat is the short for Expatriate (Adj)
Definition: denoting or relating to a person living outside their native country.
Synonyms: emigrant, living abroad, working abroad, non-native
Usage: expatriate workers.
63). Rival (Noun)
Definition: a person or thing competing with another for the same objective or for superiority in the same field of activity.
Synonyms: competitor, opponent, contestant
Usage: He has no serious rival for the job.
64). Cuddly (Adj)
Definition: endearing and pleasant to cuddle, especially as a result of being soft or plump.

Synonyms: huggable, cuddlesome; plump, curvaceous, rounded
Usage: She was short and cuddly.
65). Generous (Adj)
Definition: showing a readiness to give more of something, especially money, than is strictly necessary or expected.
Synonyms: liberal, lavish, magnanimous, munificent, giving, open-handed
Usage: A generous benefactor to the University.

66). Folk (Noun)
Definition: people in general.
Synonyms: people, humans, persons, individuals
Usage: He doesn't work the same hours as ordinary folk.
67). Shun (Verb)
Definition: persistently avoid, ignore, or reject (someone or something) through antipathy or caution.
Synonyms: avoid, evade, eschew, steer clear of, shy away from, fight shy of, recoil from
Usage: He shunned fashionable society.
68). Lament (Noun)
Definition: a passionate expression of grief or sorrow.
Synonyms: wail, moan, weeping
Usage: His mother's night-long laments for his father.
69). Hastily (Adverb)
Definition: with excessive speed or urgency; hurriedly.
Synonyms: quickly, hurriedly, in a hurry, fast, swiftly, rapidly
Usage: Maybe I acted too hastily.
70). Sighs (Verb)
Definition: emit a long, deep audible breath expressing sadness, relief, tiredness, or similar.
Synonyms: breathe out, exhale; groan, moan
Usage: Harry sank into a chair and sighed with relief
71). Obliged (Verb)
Definition: make (someone) legally or morally bound to do something.
Synonyms: require, compel, bind, make, force
Usage: Doctors are obliged by law to keep patients alive while there is a chance of recovery
72). Squeeze (Verb)
Definition: firmly press (something soft or yielding), typically with one's fingers.
Synonyms: compress, press, crush, squash, pinch, nip
Usage: I squeezed the plastic bottle and sent a jet of water out of it.
73). Intensify (Verb)
Definition: become or make more intense.

Synonyms: escalate, step up, boost, increase, raise, sharpen
Usage: Henry intensified his attack on the church.
74). Distinctive (Adj)
Definition: characteristic of one person or thing, and so serving to distinguish it from others.
Synonyms: distinguishing, characteristic, typical, individual
Usage: Each subculture developed a distinctive dress style.
75). Tales (Noun)
Definition: A writ for summoning substitute jurors when the original jury has become deficient in number.
76). Lore (Noun)
Definition: a body of traditions and knowledge on a subject or held by a particular group, typically passed from person to person by word of mouth.
Synonyms: mythology, myths, legends, stories, traditions
Usage: He had a passion for Arthurian legend and lore.
77). Staunch (Adj)
Definition: (of a wall) of strong or firm construction
Usage: These staunch walls could withstand attack by cannon.
78). Stab (Verb)
Definition: thrust a knife or other pointed weapon into (someone) so as to wound or kill.
Synonyms: knife, run through, skewer, spear
Usage: He stabbed her in the stomach.
79). Ailment (Noun)
Definition: an illness, typically a minor one.
Synonyms: illness, disease, disorder, sickness
Usage: The doctor diagnosed a common stomach ailment.
80). Overhaul (Verb)
Definition: take apart (a piece of machinery or equipment) in order to examine it and repair it if necessary.
Synonyms: service, maintain, repair, mend, fix up, patch up
Usage: The steering box was recently overhauled.
81). Sluggish (Adj)
Definition: slow-moving or inactive.
Synonyms: inactive, quite, slow, depressed
Usage: The sluggish global economy.
82). Rut (Noun)
Definition: a long deep track made by the repeated passage of the wheels of vehicles.
Synonyms: wheel track, groove, track, trough
Usage: The Land Rover bumped across the ruts.
83). Deem (Verb)
Definition: regard or consider in a specified way.

Synonyms: regard as, consider, judge, adjudge, hold to be
Usage: Many of these campaigns have been deemed successful.
84). Sprout (Verb)
Definition: grow (plant shoots or hair).
Synonyms: grow, develop; send forth, put forth
Usage: Many black cats sprout a few white hairs.
85). Gobble up (Verb)
Definition: use a large amount of (something) very quickly.
Usage: These old houses just gobble up money.
86). Lean (Verb)
Definition: be in or move into a sloping position.
Synonyms: slant, incline, bend, tilt, be at an angle
Usage: A line of palm trees leaning in the wind.
87). Heft (Verb)
Definition: lift or carry (something heavy).
Synonyms: lift, lift up, raise, raise up, heave, hoist
Usage: He lifted crates and hefted boxes.
88). Barge (Verb)
Definition: move forcefully or roughly.
Synonyms: push, shove, force, elbow, shoulder
Usage: He barged his way to the front of the queue.
89). Grasp (Verb)
Definition: seize and hold firmly.
Synonyms: grip, clutch, clasp, hold, clench, lay hold of
Usage: She grasped his hands.
90). Vow (Verb)
Definition: solemnly promise to do a specified thing.
Synonyms: swear, swear/state under oath, swear on the Bible, take an oath, pledge
Usage: The rebels vowed to continue fighting.
91). Coddle (Verb)
Definition: treat (someone) in an indulgent or overprotective way.
Synonyms: wait on someone hand and foot, cater to someone's every whim; spoil, indulge
Usage: Don't coddle repeat offenders—some of them prefer jail.
92). Bewildering (Adj)
Definition: confusing or perplexing.
Usage: There is a bewildering array of holidays to choose from.
93). Aggravate (Verb)
Definition: make (a problem, injury, or offence) worse or more serious.
Usage: Military action would only aggravate the situation.
94). Conservative (Adj)
Definition: averse to change or innovation and holding traditional values.
Synonyms: traditional, stable, unchanging

Usage: They were held in check by the conservative trade-union movement.
95). Afoot (Adverb & Adj)
Definition: in preparation or progress; happening or beginning to happen
Synonyms: going on, happening, around, about, abroad, circulating
Usage: Plans are afoot for a festival.
96). Oligarch (Noun)
Definition: a ruler in an oligarchy, (especially in Russia) a very rich business leader with a great deal of political influence.
97). Peer (Verb)
Definition: look with difficulty or concentration at someone or something.
Synonyms: squint, look closely/earnestly, try to see, look through narrowed eyes
Usage: He swivelled his head to peer in our direction.
98). Outpace (Verb)
Definition: go, rise, or improve faster than.
Usage: He outpaced all six defenders.
99). Hail (Verb) past tense: hailed; past participle: hailed
Definition: (of a large number of objects) fall or be hurled forcefully.
Synonyms: beat, shower, rain, fall, pour, drop; pelt, pepper, batter, bombard
Usage: Missiles and bombs hail down from the sky.
100). Distinction (Noun)
Definition: a difference or contrast between similar things or people.
Synonyms: difference, contrast, dissimilarity, dissimilitude, divergence
Usage: There is a sharp distinction between domestic politics and international politics.

***

Introduction

Non-English learners and aspirants often feel difficulties in pronunciation English words properly with needful tunings. These difficulties often become a serious obstacle while some English people go on trying to establish communication with them. Due to such difficulties also they often become disqualified in proving their capabilities of doing something fruitful.

This workbook and practice manual will provide the an ample scope of gaining adequate skill and competence in linguistic communication. Stress is implied in the portions related to grammar and composition of the language so as to enhance the related skills and competences of the fellow learner.

It is also recommended that one should go on practicing related exercises alonside the referral readings for the purose of gaining proficiency. A discussion on the common mistakes related to the grammar and composition of this language is also included for the purpose of drawing attention of fellow students and aspirants towards the content areas of the communication techniques.

English as a language came to India along with the colonial rule. They people felt it necessary to educate a considerable part of Indian as well as Asian communities in English for ensuring their service lines in the colonies. It was more perfectly pitched in through religious propagations.

People of India accepted the language gladly and started getting adjusted with the cultural bands of English orientation. This West Germanic language is developed from Anglo-Frician dialects.[2] This dialect is brought to Britain during 6th to 7th Century by Anglo-Saxon[3] Migrants. In due course of time this language developed considerably and transformed into the dialect of modern time.[4]

Anglo –Saxon dialect was more commonly known as old-english.[5] Near about 400 Latin loan Words[6] were introduced in English alongside the advent of Christianity. During the development Middle English near about 10,000 loan words from French origin[7] entered the English dialect and made it an enriched one.

Fully developed English dictionary, the Dictionary of the English Language, was published by Samuel Johnson in 1755. English Grammar by Pristle[8] was an added contribution in the line of development of English Language. In modern time the total English speaking community worldwide may exceed 1.5 billion mark![9] There are several other instances to

---

[2] *The Anglo-Frisian languages are the Anglic and Frisian varieties of West Germanic languages. The Northumbrian Language Society also considers Northumbrian a separate Anglic language.*

[3] *The Anglo-Saxon settlement of Britain is the process which changed the language and culture of most of what became England from Romano-British to Germanic. The Germanic-speakers in Britain, themselves of diverse origins, eventually developed a common cultural identity as Anglo-Saxons.*

[4] *Burke, Susan E (1998). ESL: Creating a quality English as a second language program: A guide for churches. Grand Rapids, Michigan: CRC Publications. ISBN 9781562123437.*

[5] *Shore, Thomas William (1906), Origin of the Anglo-Saxon Race - A Study of the Settlement of England and the Tribal Origin of the Old English People (1st ed.), London, pp. 3, 393*

[6] *English is a Germanic language, with a grammar and a core vocabulary inherited from Proto-Germanic. However, a significant portion of the English vocabulary comes from Romance and Latinate sources. A portion of these borrowings come directly from Latin,*

[7] *Baugh, Albert and Cable, Thomas. 2002. The History of the English Language. Upper Saddle River, New Jersey: Prentice Hall. pp. 158-178.*

[8] *Joseph Priestley was an English chemist, natural philosopher, separatist theologian, grammarian, multi-subject educator, and liberal political theorist who published over 150 works.*

[9] *Algeo, John. 2010. The Origins and Development of the English Language. Boston, MA: Wadsworth. pp. 182-187.*

ascertain the fact regarding the ever increasing popularity of the International Language. It has also secured a prominent position in the international arena as a common dialect that people can opt with an ease.

After becoming assured about the ever increasing popularity of this language we can now imply adequate focus on the development of skills and competence of our fellow students and aspirants through exposing them to the horizon of interactive related to perfect and advanced English dialect. We also expect a timely participation of fellow scholars in this effort. They can continue evaluating their own skills through learning continuity supplemented with self-paced evaluations.

Evolution of English Pronoun is another additional advantage of the modern English. Conflated forms of pronouns are also called an objective case. Development of such name is only because it is used only for objects of verbs. Once in old English there was distinct case system for both accusative and dative purposes. Later on such system collapsed into a single system of object (oblique) case having utility for objects of either a verb or a preposition. Studies in English were introduced in different universities during 19th and 20th Century because of its continuous developments in non-European continents. Development of such study was remarkably high in USA during 1970s. [10] It was also due to incorporation of English as another official language in most of the countries in the world.

Different courses in English are meant for different purposes. Studies in English are further accelerated with the advent of Informatics and allied fields. We consider English as a second language (a language study meant for non-English person). Errors in English are mainly observed from the field of syntax error, vocabulary error and error related to punctuations. Rules in English are periodically introduced by different scholars time to time. Not to terminate a sentence by preposition, for an example, was another rule introduced by *Robert Lowth*[11] .

While speaking or writing we all start exploring collection of words for selecting some of words having adequate capabilities of expressing our views. There are more than a collection of 220,000 words in the recent editions of the large dictionaries, but the only feeble part of this number will suffice for all our wants and aspirations. Some other words are there having a space in novels, stories and poems.
To use a big word or a foreign word when a small one and a familiar one will fulfill the same purpose along with adequate ease is a sign of ignorance. One should not go on with an exhibitionism while speaking in public or representing any note in a seminar.

All the words incorporated in the English language are basically divided into nine great classes. These classes are called in general the Parts of Speech [Article, Noun, Adjective, Pronoun, Verb, Adverb, Preposition, Conjunction and Interjection]. Of these, the Noun, the group of naming words, is the most important, as all the others are more or less remain dependent upon it. A Noun signifies the name of any person, place or thing, thoughts, ideas name of any other kinds. Things of which we can have either thought or idea in our mind is grouped under the head Noun. There are two kinds of Nouns: Proper and Common. Common Nouns are names which belong in common to a race or class (For Example man, city, animal, mountain etc). Proper Nouns distinguish individual members of a race or class (For example John, Philadelphia, Himalaya). Naming words are of varying types and are used differently at different places.

Chandan Sukumar Sengupta

***

---

[10] *National Center for Education Statistics (January 1993). "120 Years of American Education: A Statistical Portrait" (PDF). National Center for Education Statistics. Retrieved September 12, 2018.*
[11] *Robert Lowth (26 March 1794). A Short Introduction to English Grammar: With Critical Notes. Printed for J.J . Tourneisin – via Internet Archive.*

1. Application of Basic Rules

Set 1

1. Food prices have been … steadily for at least ten years.
a) rising
b) lifting
c) raising

2. I'll have to study hard, … I can pass the exam.
a) so that
b) such
c) in order

3. You … to eat if you are not hungry.
a) needn't
b) haven't
c) don't have

4. We'll dance and … we'll have lunch.
a) straight away
b) so
c) then

5. She has to go to Germany for the next … of the training.
a) step
b) stage
c) point

6. When the meeting had finished, we went … the plan once again.
a) up
b) down
c) over

7. I locked the animals in the cage to … them from getting away.
a) avoid
b) hinder
c) prevent

8. You're … your time trying to persuade her.
a) wasting
b) losing
c) missing

9. Our last cook was better than our … one.
a) latter
b) instant
c) current

10. I am grateful to Mary for being so patient … us.
a) for
b) with
c) at

11. Have you exchanged that lovely car … this?
a) with
b) by
c) for

12. The weather was … the poor harvest.
a) condemned for
b) found fault with for
c) blamed for

13. Olivia is teaching three classes and she is examining at a literature exam tomorrow. …, she is chairing a meeting at the Bright Owl Club.
a) On top of it
b) At top
c) On the top of it

14. I don't see any … in arriving early at the show.
a) cause
b) point
c) reason

15. Your application for a vise was turned … by the consulate.
a) aside
b) over
c) down

16. Shopping malls account for 70 percent of the retail business in this country because they are controlled environments which … concerns about the weather.
a) justify

b) foster

c) eliminate

17. It is … impossible to tell the twins apart.

a) virtually

b) closely

c) extremely

18. The man claimed that he was the … heir to the throne.

a) due

b) correct

c) rightful

19. The rather humid climate in no way … from the beauty of these places.

a) protracts

b) detracts

c) attracts

20. … no need to buy traveller's cheques.

a) It's

b) It has

c) There's

21. Is there … bread for all the sandwiches?

a) enough

b) plenty

c) equal

22. Teaching is not a/an … which pays very well.

a) work

b) post

c) occupation

23. This letter didn't come through the post. It was delivered personally, … hand.

a) from

b) by

c) with

24. I … do that if I were you.

a) shan't

b) won't

c) wouldn't

25. There was nothing to … her with the burglary until the police found two gold ring in her car.

a) link

b) place

c) join

26. The manufacturers are advertising a new … of perfume.

a) mark

b) pack

c) brand

27. … my stay in hospital, I lost three kilos.

a) During

b) On

c) In

28. I'm sorry to hear that they have … . They were good friends.

a) dropped out

b) fallen out

c) dropped against

29. Shall I use this … to fry the eggs?

a) dish

b) tin

c) pan

30. She … being given a receipt for the bill she had paid.

a) insisted on

b) demanded

c) asked to

31. These cars historically had two doors but the latest … has four.

a) brand

b) mark

c) model

32. That girl is far ahead … everyone else in the class.

a) of

b) with

c) from

33. She is also interested … art.

a) with

b) in

c) about

34. It's impossible to prevent the boys from quarreling … each other.
a) for
b) with
c) by
35. I'm thinking … looking for a new job in another city.
a) on
b) at
c) of
36. Steve prefers football … tennis.
a) to
b) over
c) than
37. The experience in a psychiatric ward … for the rest of his life.
a) had an influence on him
b) had influence on him
c) had an influence at him
38. If I had known the way to her house, I … her last Monday afternoon.
a) have been visiting
b) had been visiting
c) would have visited
39. He ... that he had been involved in the decision.
a) refused
b) declined
c) denied
40. As brown as … . This phrase means having a tanned skin after sunbathing.
a) dust
b) a berry
c) chocolate
41. It's an awful … your friend couldn't come.
a) shame
b) sorrow
c) shock
42. There is a problem at our TV station. Please do not … your set.
a) repair
b) change
c) adjust
43. Be careful! The cat may … you.
a) kick
b) scratch
c) tear
44. They agreed to … the question of payment.
a) discuss
b) control
c) increase
45. Owing to the bad weather, the garden party was … .
a) shouted off
b) spoken against
c) called off
46. I am sorry I opened your bag but I … it for mine.
a) confused
b) imagined
c) mistook
47. The … of these volunteers for hard work is remarkable.
a) ability
b) efficiency
c) capacity
48. I like this country, but I wish it … rain quite so much.
a) won't
b) didn't
c) hasn't
49. She was so tired that she … asleep in the chair.
a) fell
b) went
c) became
50. Mike has just taken an examination … chemistry.
a) on
b) in
c) for

51. They shouldn't have … the incident. It wasn't my fault.

a) accused me of

b) blamed me for

c) blamed me

52. They won't lend you the money without some … that you will pay it back.

a) profit

b) charge

c) guarantee

53. When you come tomorrow why not … your brother with you?

a) carry

b) bring

c) fetch

54. After she had broken her leg, Marry could only go up and down stairs … .

a) with difficulty

b) in difficulties

c) hardly

55. Who does this laptop belong … ?

a) for

b) with

c) to

56. All her handbags … of leather.

a) being made

b) are made

c) had been made

57. John is the perfect person to take on this difficult job. He's a really hard-… person and won't stand for any nonsense.

a) ship

b) nosed

c) bargain

58. What does a sabbatical year mean?

a) a miserable year

b) a year in which previously made plans are bound to

c) a year in which one is released from one's normal duties

59. It always … me as odd that she should go to work so late in the day.

a) hit

b) smacked

c) struck

60. I walked away as calmly as I could … they thought I was the thief.

a) in case

b) or else

c) to avoid

61. If it's raining tomorrow, we shall have to … the match till Sunday.

a) cancel

b) put off

c) put away

62. Call in and see our … of spring fashions today.

a) reputation

b) election

c) selection

63. We have no … in our files of your recent letters to the company.

a) record

b) account

c) list

64. When her aunt dies, she … a lot of money.

a) earned

b) inherited

c) paid

65. Give him a telephone number to ring … he gets lost.

a) whether

b) unless

c) in case

66. Her parents never allowed her … .

a) smoking

b) a smoking

c) to smoke

67. Bill is only interested … making money.

a) in

b) about

c) on

68. The boy was very upset by the … of his English examination.

a) failure
b) result
c) effect
69. Their actions caused the rate of inflation to
… sharply.
a) lift
b) raise
c) rise
70. They were good friends. I was surprised
when they … .
a) fell out
b) fell off
c) fell down
71. I had to leave early … I didn't feel very
well.
a) too
b) because
c) also
72. After closing the envelope, the assistant
manager … the stamps on
firmly.
a) licked
b) stuck
c) struck
73. Don't be so sure … yourself! You might be
wrong.
a) on
b) from
c) of
74. This book will prove useful … you.
a) for
b) to
c) on
75. You should not be so sensitive … criticism.
a) to
b) at
c) on

76. I am not familiar … his novels.
a) with
b) about
c) for

77. You should study the college … for full
particulars of enrolment.
a) prospect
b) syllabus
c) prospectus
78. A novel is a form of … which may include
many facts.
a) short story
b) legend
c) fiction
79. The relationship that matters most in the life
of a … is the one between
him and his constituency party, they say.
a) judge
b) politician
c) captain
80. The case of the missing millionaire has
become the … of considerable
interest in the press.
a) focus
b) middle
c) target
81. These people are thought … less friendly
than people from our country.
a) been
b) being
c) to be
82. Would you give this report to Mr. Smith?
Sorry, I can't. He doesn't … .
a) any more work here
b) work any more here
c) work here any longer
83. After hitting her arm, she had a large black
… .
a) bruise
b) cut
c) swelling

84. This is not the right … to ask for my help; I
am away on business.
a) situation
b) moment
c) opportunity

85. I hadn't seen him for years, but when I saw him in the street, I … him at
once.
a) reminded
b) realized
c) remembered

86. The dog was so frightened that it ran … the bed to hide.
a) along
b) beside
c) under

87. John was unable to … my party as he was ill.
a) visit
b) attend
c) be present

88. Jane bought red shoes to … her red dress.
a) match
b) pair
c) mate

89. We'll have to … the meeting until next month.
a) put down
b) put off
c) put round

90. I am not sure … the black coat is.
a) whom
b) who
c) whose

91. I don't think he'll beat the opponent. He's out of … .
a) fitness
b) practice
c) play

92. She is a very … person, but she has no sense of humour.
a) pleasant

b) amusing
c) enjoyable

93. The university arranges a … to Madrid every year.
a) travel

b) rout
c) trip

94. Beware … these people.
a) from
b) of
c) at

95. If you fail … this attempt, don't count on me for help.
a) on
b) at
c) in

96. I separated them … each other because they were fighting.
a) of
b) from
c) against

97. I have to leave before six and so … .
a) do you
b) leave you
c) you do

98. There were no lifeboats on the little ship because it was … to be
unsinkable.
a) claimed
b) told
c) believed

99. This church was … by a famous architect.
a) outlined
b) designed
c) produced

100. Mary is plain, but her sister is very … .
a) attractive
b) complex
c) sympathetic

101. Her boyfriend treated her badly. I'm surprised she … it for so long.
a) put off
b) put through
c) put up with

102. The manager … me to open a deposit account.
a) warned
b) approved

c) advised
103. This organization tries to send food to countries where people are suffering … malnutrition.
a) from
b) for
c) by
104. If they are to understand the notice, the instructions must be … clearer.
a) wrote
b) made
c) done
105. … you like what I want to do or not, you won't make me change my mind regarding this situation.
a) If
b) When
c) Whether
106. Doctors usually have to study for at least eight years before becoming fully … .
a) tested
b) proved
c) qualified
107. The weather was pleasant with … a gentle wind to cool us down.
a) just
b) almost
c) nearly
108. I wish you wouldn't … your clothes all over the room.
a) sprawl
b) scatter
c) straggle

109. … she had no money for a bus, Olive had to walk all the way home.
a) As
b) For
c) Thus
110. I didn't want to make up my mind until I had heard her … of the story.
a) angle

b) edge
c) side
111. It's strange that Jane is as … as her mother is beautiful.
a) dull
b) plain
c) raw
112. Since the accident he has been walking with a … .
a) slope
b) lame
c) limp
113. I flew to the island, then … a car for five days and visited most places.
a) charged
b) bought
c) hired
114. In Russia, surgeons have given a man a/an … heart.
a) artificial
b) unreal
c) false
115. The examiners had to … most of the candidates.
a) fire
b) fail
c) fall
116. Our company made a record … last year.
a) benefit
b) wage
c) profit
117. They must economize … fuel.
a) on

b) in
c) with
118. When I understood what she was saying, everything … .
a) fell into the place
b) fell into place
c) fell off the place
119. I had to give a full … of my car when I reported it stolen.

a) detail

b) account

c) description

120. His version of the facts doesn't … with the version I heard from Jane.

a) accord

b) argue

c) amount

121. They have … to accommodate us and the children too.

a) such a small house

b) too small a house

c) a too small house

122. After they had … the carpet, the employees went back to the office.

a) laid

b) lain

c) lied

123. It will … be Christmas again.

a) fast

b) next

c) soon

124. Be careful not to … your coffee on this rug.

a) drip

b) spill

c) filter

125. Mary had to leave her family … when she went abroad to work.

a) at all costs

b) out

c) behind

Set 2

126. Metal … at high temperatures.

a) grows

b) expands

c) enlarges

127. Because of the poor harvest, cereals prices have … in the last three months.

a) gone up

b) jumped up

c) sprung up

128. I'm … worried about Mary; she always seems to be exhausted.

a) as

b) such

c) so

129. I have difficulty … without glasses.

a) read

b) of reading

c) in reading

130. He arrived rather late. The party was already … .

a) in full swing

b) at full tilt

c) in full bloom

131. My neighbour plays his records … in his flat at night and nobody can get enough sleep.

a) at full tilt

b) at full blast

c) in full cry

132. It's unwise to … in a quarrel between husbands.

a) involve

b) poke

c) interfere

133. I will … the project with other members and see what they think about it.

a) discuss

b) talk

c) explain

134. The poor farmer was very angry … the dogs chasing his sheep.

a) about

b) because

c) with

135. I think she's quite honest … her intentions.
a) about
b) with
c) in
136. I will be waiting … them at the entrance door.
a) on
b) for
c) at
137. It's no use complaining … the cold during winter.
a) of
b) from
c) on
138. Manufacturers are now … of the latest credit restrictions.
a) smelling the rat
b) feeling the pinch
c) cooking the books
139. This music type is an American art form which is now … in Europe
through the efforts of expatriates.
a) foundering
b) waning
c) flourishing
140. She was … disappointed when she learned that she hadn't got the job
she dreamt of.
a) fully
b) highly
c) bitterly
141. They have … the castle and it is now a luxury hotel.
a) undone
b) remade
c) transformed

142. I … so much last night: I feel terrible.
a) shouldn't have eaten
b) mustn't have eaten
c) didn't have to eat
143. The man stole one of the officers' uniforms and managed to escape by

passing himself … as a guard.
a) out
b) off
c) through
144. … we set off in the next minutes, we'll be there on time.
a) In case
b) So long
c) Provided
145. If he drinks any more beer, I don't think he'll be … to football this
afternoon.
a) skilled
b) capable
c) fit
146. My manager's … of my work doesn't matter to me at all.
a) opinion
b) belief
c) meaning
147. The recent … domestic violence is worrying the police.
a) increase in
b) increase of
c) increase about
148. There's … to hurry.
a) no purpose
b) no need
c) impossible
149. The officers … the kidnapper from escaping by blocking all exits.
a) allowed
b) avoided
c) prevented

150. This meat isn't suitable … .
a) the grill
b) for grilling
c) being grilled
151. A bridge is already … over the river.
a) being built
b) erecting
c) been erected

152. The painting is …; the thief will be disappointed.
a) invalid
b) priceless
c) worthless

153. Even though he is thirty-three, he lives … his mother's salary.
a) from
b) at
c) on

154. It should be obvious … you that this problem will be solved.
a) for
b) to
c) at

155. Mike often forgets to do what he has been told and is scolded for being … .
a) rebellious
b) malicious
c) disobedient

156. The house is quite warm. The oil heater gives … .
a) out a good heat
b) off a good heat
c) out good heat

157. In the middle of my trip I stopped … a rest on the river bank.
a) have
b) to have
c) having

158. After ruling that the article had unjustly … the reputation of the
businessman, the judge ordered the magazine to … its libelous statements

in print.
a) praised…publicize
b) injured…retract
c) sullied…communicate

159. When she heard the news she went completely … .
a) fuse

b) thunder
c) spare

160. I won't … those children making a noise in my apartment!
a) have
b) allow
c) let

161. It's great that your father managed to … that man. Somehow he had
deceived many people.
a) see to
b) see through
c) see out

162. My car is much older … than yours.
a) form
b) manufacture
c) model

163. I … in bed all night thinking about it.
a) laid
b) led
c) lay

164. According to the medical doctor, there's absolutely nothing the … with
you.
a) wrong
b) matter
c) problem

165. I looked everywhere but I couldn't find … at all.
a) anyone
b) no one
c) someone

166. It was … a simple question that everyone answered it.
a) much
b) such
c) too

167. I like my eggs soft …, not hard.
a) cooked
b) steamed
c) boiled

168. I was utterly amazed when the train arrived exactly … time.
a) on
b) by
c) in

169. I'd like to take this … of wishing you all the best.
a) chance
b) opportunity
c) occasion

170. Learners of English may fail to .. between unfamiliar sounds.
a) separate
b) differ
c) distinguish

171. … her opinion, English cheese is better than French cheese.
a) To
b) By
c) In

172. Their parents would not ... them to go there for the weekend.
a) agree
b) permit
c) consent

173. Every Sunday the old man's dog goes to the shop to … him a
newspaper.
a) carry
b) fetch
c) take

174. It's late! It's time we … .
a) are gone

b) are going
c) were gone

175. I drove around the area for half an hour but I couldn't find a car … .
a) park
b) plan
c) garage

176. The smell was so bad that it … me off my food.

a) took
b) put
c) got

177. Although she hasn't said anything she … to be upset about it.
a) seems
b) acts
c) behaves

178. It's strange: his sister is blonde, … he is very dark.
a) therefore
b) however
c) whereas

179. I very much … that you will come to dinner next Monday.
a) hope
b) want
c) wish

180. Crops are sometimes completely destroyed by … of locusts.
a) bands
b) swarms
c) flocks

181. There's something wrong with my watch: it has … five minutes in the
last hour.
a) gained
b) won
c) advanced

182. Keep in mind that if you are … to customers, they'll walk out of the
shop.
a) brush

b) rough
c) rude

183. The air in the house felt cold and … after some days of bad weather.
a) wet
b) damp
c) moist

184. Do you want to wait for a table at this restaurant or shall we go …

else?
a) anywhere
b) everywhere
c) somewhere
185. Children who use escalators should always be accompanied … an
adult.
a) with
b) by
c) beside
186. I took someone else's coat by … .
a) fortune
b) error
c) mistake
187. How long does it … to get home in the morning?
a) take you
b) need you
c) demand
188. It's becoming more and more … that the Government has lost its
confidence.
a) apparent
b) expected
c) anticipated
189. You need a special … to go into this building.
a) agreement
b) allowance
c) permit
190. I don't like her, so I have no intention … speaking to her.
a) about

b) of
c) with
191. I had to drive carefully because the road was icy in several … .
a) places
b) blocks
c) pieces
192. Don't invite him; I can't stand his bad … .
a) mood

b) mind
c) temper
193. Not only … the movie, but she had also read the book.
a) she did see
b) she saw
c) had she seen
194. I had a meeting at work which went … much longer than I expected.
a) in
b) on
c) by
195. Tom … me to take a lawyer to court with me.
a) suggested
b) insisted
c) advised
196. Poor woman! She has so much to cope … .
a) with
b) in
c) by
197. Tim has always gone … strange hobbies like inventing secret codes.
a) by
b) into
c) in for
198. As he is an expert, his opinions would be worth … .
a) to have
b) having
c) of having

199. Nowhere … this room.
a) is as cold as in
b) is it as cold as
c) it is as cold as in
200. There's just something about him that really puts my … up.
a) handle
b) teeth
c) back
201. The explorer walked all the way along the river, from its mouth to its

… .
a) cause
b) source
c) well
202. She soon received promotion, for her superiors realised that she was a woman of considerable … .
a) ability
b) future
c) possibility
203. It is … knowledge that they quarrel violently several times a month.
a) complete
b) normal
c) common
204. After his mother died, he was … up by his grandparents.
a) taken
b) brought
c) grown
205. You should do something worthwhile with your time instead of … it!
a) spending
b) using
c) wasting
206. The police have issued … to local citizens to be on the lookout for thieves.
a) warnings
b) advice
c) information

207. If you require any more … about the event, please telephone us.
a) news
b) fact
c) information
208. Wait … you get at the office before you unpack this.
a) when
b) until
c) after

209. The students … names appear on the list all failed the exam.
a) whose
b) which
c) their
210. When the police appealed for witnesses, many people came … .
a) across
b) on
c) forward
211. Can you give me a rough … of how much it will cost?
a) esteem
b) value
c) estimate
212. I do play billiards, but I … tennis.
a) prefer
b) like
c) would rather
213. The consultant gave me … useful information.
a) one
b) some
c) the
214. One of the … has fallen off the clock.
a) hands
b) pointers
c) arms
215. How old do you have to be … you can drive a car in your country?
a) when
b) since
c) before
216. I'll let you have the book back next Friday without … .
a) miss
b) fail
c) doubt
217. … I ask him for money he owes me, he says he will bring it in a few weeks.
a) However

b) Whatever

c) Whenever

218. I … to inform you that we cannot exchange articles.

a) resent

b) regret

c) sense

219. I am responsible … what has happened.

a) with

b) for

c) by

220. They have to arrange for the … of their furniture accessories.

a) sole

b) sale

c) seal

221. The boy wouldn't go into the sea … his parents went too.

a) unless

b) except

c) but

222. The … part of the week is always busy for Steven.

a) start

b) near

c) early

223. I … to take my neighbour to court if he didn't stop making so much noise.

a) offered

b) suggested

c) threatened

224. It wasn't his … that he was late.

a) blame

b) fault

c) error

225. She sat there with her arms … doing nothing.

a) turned

b) folded

c) twisted

226. Our neighbours … their hedge cut once a year.

a) have

b) do

c) make

227. I could tell she was pleased … the expression on his face.

a) at

b) by

c) for

228. Steve calls himself Steve Milton, but his … surname is Smith.

a) natural

b) current

c) real

229. If you keep trying you might … to do it.

a) succeed

b) manage

c) understand

230. Their child was born in the ambulance … to the hospital.

a) on the way

b) by the way

c) a long way

231. The meeting is now … .

a) on end

b) at the end

c) at an end

232. She promised to write … I never heard from her again.

a) except

b) but

c) because

233. I … to Tim for my bad behaviour.

a) coped

b) excused

c) apologised

234. Ever … she was in school she has wanted to become a medical doctor.

a) since

b) always

c) after

235. The bottle was on the top shelf, out of … .
a) achievement
b) arrival
c) reach

236. Laptops are supposed to … time, but I'm not so sure they do!
a) spare
b) save
c) waste

237. I didn't mean to do it; it was … accident.
a) in
b) on
c) by

238. His speech was …, eliciting thunderous applause.
a) tedious
b) cowardly
c) well-received

239. What does "a wild goose chase" mean?
a) a wild night on the town
b) a search for something that cannot be found
c) a dangerous race in the streets between cars

240. You should have avoided risking …, General!
a) the lives of your soldiers

b) your soldiers' life
c) the life of your soldiers'

241. … goes the train; now we will have to walk!
a) On time
b) There
c) At once

242. Jane is important to him. He wouldn't get … without her.
a) by
b) over
c) round

Set 3

243. They live in the house … the blue door.

a) which
b) where
c) with

244. I phoned the bank to … how much money I had to pay.
a) control
b) check
c) test

245. His parents give him anything he wants and as a result he's very … .
a) ruined
b) spoilt
c) damaged

246. … I am studying at the best university and I hope to get a job soon.
a) In a moment
b) At present
c) At this instant

247. He is a fast typist but his letters are full of spelling … .
a) mistakes
b) wrongs
c) faults

248. The officers have asked that … who saw the accident should inform
them.
a) one
b) someone
c) anyone

249. If the greengrocer has some tomatoes … buy some?
a) you will
b) would you
c) shall you

250. I will offer a small … to anyone who finds my missing cat.
a) reward
b) receipt
c) repayment

251. The party has … to win the elections.
a) achieved
b) managed

c) attained

252. You … do the washing-up: we can do it later.

a) wouldn't

b) daren't

c) needn't

253. They demand higher wages because prices are … .

a) growing

b) exceeding

c) rising

254. You should be careful when you wash this … blouse.

a) weak

b) feeble

c) sensitive

255. My parents always fall … in front of the TV.

a) asleep

b) sleepy

c) sleeping

256. You can never rely … her to be punctual.

a) of

b) with

c) on

257. Are you interested … rock music?

a) on

b) in

c) of

258. You should reply … his letter.

a) on

b) for

c) to

259. I will certainly act … your advice.

a) with

b) at

c) on

260. as sound as … . This phrase means healthy, in good condition.

a) steel

b) a monkey

c) a bell

261. Buy the … of soap which is now on sale.

a) model

b) brand

c) mark

262. My uncle took … jogging when he retired.

a) up

b) on

c) over

263. There has been a rather worrying … five per cent in our profits last year.

a) drop in

b) fall in

c) drop of

264. … you hurry, you won't catch the train.

a) Unless

b) Except

c) As

265. The customer … his money back.

a) asked

b) demanded

c) requested

266. I … him to go to the Lost Property office.

a) noticed

b) announced

c) advised

267. I couldn't resist having another slice of pizza even … I was supposed to be on diet.

a) though

b) however

c) although

268. These old buildings are going to be … soon.

a) laid out

b) run down

c) pulled down

269. … as I like ice-cream, I can't eat any more now.

a) Much

b) Even

c) So

270. You may borrow ten books, provided you show them to … is at the
desk.
a) who
b) whoever
c) whom

271. Is he playing computer games? He's … to be washing the car.
a) hoped
b) supposed
c) expected

272. Mary was angry with me for breaking the windows, but it happened …
accident.
a) by
b) in
c) on

273. The room was crowded with over fifty people … into it.
a) pushed
b) packed
c) stuck

274. Beware of the friends who appear to be enthusiastic … your success.
a) of
b) with
c) about

275. They want to watch the latest movie … TV.
a) in
b) at
c) on

276. … to leave early is rarely granted.
a) Permission
b) Leave
c) Allowance

277. …, my colleagues didn't laugh at me.
a) For my surprise
b) To my surprise
c) As to surprise me

278. If you had gone there, you … my sister.
a) would have met
b) would meet
c) had met

279. She never goes in lifts because she is terrified of … spaces.
a) constricted
b) compressed
c) contained

280. It never … to me that she would be there.
a) recurred
b) occurred
c) contemplated

281. The assistant was … helpful, but Mike felt she could have given him
more information.
a) exactly
b) totally
c) quite

282. The meal was excellent; the steak was particularly … .
a) flavoured
b) tasteful
c) delicious

283. Are there any seats left for this evening's …?
a) opera
b) act
c) performance

284. Having … the table, she called the family for supper.
a) laid
b) spread
c) ordered

285. As I have been ill, I have had no … to discuss the business plan.
a) suitability
b) possibility
c) opportunity

286. Tom … to turn up for the football match.
a) omitted
b) failed
c) stopped

287. The manager's presence was helpful, but he could … us more money.
a) give
b) gave
c) have given

288. There are five lawyers in my town and I have consulted … of them in turn.
a) every
b) each
c) any

289. The final course was so difficult that I didn't … any progress at all.
a) do
b) create
c) make

290. I'm tired of looking at ancient … .
a) ruins
b) foundations
c) remnants

291. My bike is gone: it must … .
a) have been stolen
b) have stolen
c) be stolen

292. There's a … to her patience.
a) top
b) limit
c) bottom

293. I … hands with the guests.
a) gave
b) nodded
c) shook

294. We had a great … of trouble getting through customs.
a) level
b) lot
c) deal

295. Rose trees need to be … regularly.
a) cut
b) clipped
c) pruned

296. What made you think … such a thing?
a) of
b) on
c) at

297. I would go to the pool if the weather … good.
a) is
b) were
c) has been

298. I rang you up while he … his report.
a) was finishing
b) has been finishing
c) had finished

299. The bus … is 50 cents.
a) cost
b) fare
c) charge

300. Before the invention of refrigeration, the … of meat was a problem.
a) preservation
b) keeping
c) maintenance

301. Could I have another one? Oh, there doesn't seem to be … .
a) any left
b) some left
c) left any

302. I will go on working on the farm … I can.
a) through
b) during
c) as long as

303. I'll ask Ms. Thompson to … to you as soon as she returns.
a) ring
b) contact
c) speak

304. This new model works by letting light through a small … at the front.
a) leak
b) hole
c) break

305. You will have to … your holiday if you are too ill.

a) cut down
b) call off
c) put aside

306. If you go to the market you might find a …
.
a) chance
b) bargain
c) trade

307. The train was ... by three hours because of bad weather.
a) postponed
b) put off
c) delayed

308. My guests didn't leave until 3 a.m.; they … have enjoyed themselves.
a) can't
b) must
c) might

309. She was sitting just ... Steve and John.
a) beside
b) off
c) besides

310. Mary remembered the correct address only … she had posted the letter.
a) since
b) following
c) after

311. I have never … any experience of living in a small village.
a) wished
b) made
c) had

312. I'm very … of cash at the moment.
a) down
b) empty
c) short

313. The … were told to fasten their seat belts.
a) passengers
b) flyers
c) customers

314. There are … trains running today.

a) scarcer
b) fewer
c) little

315. Mary isn't … well with the new manager.
a) going on
b) taking on
c) getting on

316. Has this idea ever occurred … you?
a) at
b) to
c) on

317. I'm … with your stupid ideas.
a) get rid
b) fed over
c) fed up

318. If they had been able … it for you, they would have helped you.
a) to do
b) doing
c) is doing

319. The officers carried out a … search for the missing diplomat.
a) through
b) thoughtful
c) thorough

320. Fitting together the fragments was a … task.
a) minute
b) minuscule
c) painstaking

321. It will … rain later so we should go now.
a) probably
b) likely
c) usually

322. I would have cleaned this mess if I … you were coming.
a) would have known
b) had known
c) have known

323. We have … to meet at the station at 8 o'clock.
a) confirmed

b) combined

c) arranged

324. There is always … traffic in the city centre.

a) full

b) strong

c) heavy

325. He's … to drink too much at parties.

a) adequate

b) apt

c) common

326. We must get there … or other.

a) somehow

b) anyhow

c) anywhere

327. She was left to make all the … for the meeting.

a) procedures

b) provisions

c) arrangements

328. The new girl … type at 45 words per minute.

a) need

b) can

c) dare

329. I'll wait over there until … ready.

a) you are

b) you will be

c) you were

330. You must move your car; … I have to give you a ticket.

a) whether

b) therefore

c) otherwise

331. A manager of a large company is given a big … .

a) money

b) pay

c) salary

332. Heavy goods delivery vehicles may not carry … of more than fifteen tons.

a) masses

b) sizes

c) loads

333. After they went on strike there was a … of water.

a) shortage

b) drain

c) loss

334. She's entitled to a pension, but she won't dream … retiring yet.

a) on

b) of

c) to

335. Mix the contents … a little water.

a) of

b) with

c) at

336. You can try … if you really need to improve your language skills.

a) listening to BBC

b) listening at BBC

c) to listening to BBC

337. His … of Alexander the Great was acclaimed as one of the best.

a) entertainment

b) portrayal

c) spectacle

338. The army … defeat at the hands of such powerful enemies.

a) bore

b) supported

c) suffered

339. Their accounts were phony. They had been cooking the … for years.

a) books

b) spinner

c) trade

Set 4

340. Practical … is desirable for candidates.

a) exploit
b) initiative
c) experience
341. The director opened the letter without … to read the address on the envelope.
a) worrying
b) bothering
c) caring

342. Hurry! She's already here. I didn't think she … till tomorrow.
a) was coming
b) is coming
c) is to come
343. If you have any … concerning this report please phone us.
a) requests
b) wishes
c) queries
344. Could you … exactly what you saw?
a) inform
b) describe
c) point
345. He has brought you a … of flowers.
a) branch
b) bunch
c) bush
346. The child seems to be incapable … keeping his room tidy.
a) at
b) with
c) of
347. In the summer I often sleep in the … air on the terrace.
a) clean
b) clear
c) open
348. This dress … you perfectly.
a) likes
b) suits
c) matches

349. I bought the phone because the colours … the colours of the car.
a) match
b) fit
c) suit
350. To promote her so quickly you must have a high … of her ability.
a) view
b) idea
c) opinion
351. We … as well go without him.
a) can
b) may
c) just
352. She … out of the window for a moment and then went on writing.
a) glanced
b) glimpsed
c) regarded
353. You should keep receipts from shops as proof … purchase.
a) to
b) for
c) of
354. Don't mention it … my girlfriend, but I paid $80 for this perfume.
a) to
b) at
c) with
355. The child knocked … the door.
a) on
b) for
c) at
356. You must have … the examination before Friday.
a) passing
b) entered for
c) sit for
357. They … for you for more than one hour now.
a) have waited
b) have been waiting

c) wait

358. I would have come home earlier if you …
me.

a) had told

b) have told

c) told

359. Petrol is so expensive … they use public
transport.

a) then

b) thus

c) that

360. There has been some … in their bilateral
relations.

a) destitution

b) deterioration

c) depreciation

361. They take too much … of his kindness.

a) profit

b) use

c) advantage

362. I can easily … you up for the night.

a) put

b) take

c) keep

363. My car is very old, but I can't … to buy a
new one.

a) achieve

b) reach

c) afford

364. Two passengers were killed and the other
was … injured.

a) hardly

b) severely

c) unusually

365. After ten years the bedroom wallpaper had
considerably … .

a) faded

b) mixed

c) lighted

366. My attempt to pass the final exam was … .

a) unmerciful

b) unhelpful

c) unsuccessful

367. She … at the Latin College for French.

a) enlisted

b) inscribed

c) enrolled

368. I admit I suffer from a … of patience with
old people.

a) lack

b) limit

c) shortage

369. The building is in good … though it needs
to be painted.

a) state

b) condition

c) position

370. I can't be sure I'll be there in time. I … be
late.

a) should

b) must

c) may

371. His suit didn't … him properly.

a) meet

b) fit

c) frame

372. She may be quick … understanding, but
she's not capable of doing it.

a) at

b) in

c) for

373. We have some important business to attend
… .

a) with

b) at

c) to

374. Steve, you should not boast … your
success.

a) of

b) with

c) from

375. I'm sorry, I haven't got … change.

a) all

b) any

c) lots

376. An oppressive ..., and not the festive mood characterized the mood of
the gathering.
a) senility
b) inanity
c) solemnity

377. I think it's ... your luck to drive without a license.
a) risking
b) tempting
c) pushing

378. If you looked back far enough, you would see that you are ... related
to Karl Marx.
a) distantly
b) slightly
c) previously

379. I can't understand it; your handwriting is
... .
a) illegible
b) illicit
c) illusive

380. Hello! You ... be the new employee.
a) could
b) should
c) must

381. Last year the cereals harvest was disappointing, but this year it looks
as if we shall have a better ... .
a) crop
b) amount
c) product

382. She was in ... of a large number of men.
a) direction
b) leadership
c) charge

383. Tom was born during the last war, which would ... him about 50 now.
a) give
b) make
c) calculate

384. The actor never married, choosing to remain ... all his life.
a) separate
b) single
c) individual

385. The consultant showed me ... the washing machine.
a) the working of
b) to work
c) how to use

386. The driver failed to signal his ... to turn left.
a) idea
b) purpose
c) intention

387. I wish you wouldn't call her ... that name.
a) by
b) with
c) under

388. I had ... reached the park when I saw everyone leaving.
a) quite
b) almost
c) rather

389. She tried to ... to see him at least once a week.
a) call up
b) come on
c) drop in

390. No, Kate isn't stupid. ..., she's rather clever.
a) Now
b) Currently
c) Actually

391. The Minister resigned as a/an ... of the incident.
a) effect
b) result
c) cause

392. The names of the winners will be ... in the next magazine issue.
a) told

b) informed

c) announced

393. When the clock … twelve, I left.

a) struck

b) beat

c) shot

394. The store is only open … weekday mornings now.

a) for

b) in

c) on

395. They think he is very good … drawing.

a) at

b) for

c) in

396. Every day thousands of … fly the Atlantic for negotiations.

a) dealers

b) merchants

c) businessmen

397. Prices continued to rise … the ruling party became unpopular.

a) on condition that

b) with the result that

c) on the chance that

398. I would help the old lady in her shopping if she … me.

a) will ask

b) ask

c) asked

399. … for a trip last Friday?

a) Did you go

b) Will you go

c) Have you gone

400. The child was taught that it was … to interrupt.

a) coarse

b) rude

c) crude

401. She was … better than her brother at chess.

a) miles

b) feet

c) inches

402. I often speak to her on my … to work.

a) travel

b) way

c) road

403. The noise prevented me from … to sleep.

a) starting

b) going

c) beginning

404. This horse is famous for … the National race two times.

a) gaining

b) conquering

c) winning

405. Before starting a new chapter, I'd like to … what we discussed yesterday.

a) run up

b) run along

c) run through

406. I think it's time we … on our way.

a) are

b) were

c) will be

407. Would you … taking care of the cat for two hours?

a) mind

b) matter

c) agree

408. The world record for this event is almost impossible to … .

a) beat

b) meet

c) compare

409. We've been … with this business partner for many years.

a) competing

b) shopping

c) dealing

410. She applied for training as a pilot, but they turned her … .

a) down
b) over
c) back
411. The child wasn't accustomed … by coach.
a) travel
b) to travel
c) to travelling
412. She has left her phone at home. She's
always so … .
a) forgetful
b) forgotten
c) forgetting
413. Newly-… coins always look clean.
a) moulded
b) minted
c) printed
414. I had to go to the library to … some books.
a) give
b) return
c) buy
415. It was such a hot day … the surface of the
material was damaged.
a) as
b) so
c) that
416. She always … out in a crowd because of
her style.
a) stood
b) found
c) looked
417. Please apply … the secretary for this type
of information.
a) for
b) at
c) to

418. Though the concert had been enjoyable, it
was overly … .
a) sublime
b) protracted
c) extensive
419. A skillful …, John adopted a posture of
patience and … toward the

protestors.
a) academician/understanding
b) pundit/tolerance
c) negotiator/compromise
420. Could you give me a rough … of the costs?
a) estimate
b) value
c) correlation
421. There is a … of $2,000 for information
leading to the thief.
a) gift
b) reward
c) prize
422. The manager didn't pay for the meal
himself – he put it on his
company's … account.
a) expense
b) price
c) value
423. I knew her … we were young.
a) until
b) as
c) when
424. I … them run away from the bank.
a) allowed
b) saw
c) felt
425. I only have … days left in Spain.
a) little
b) a few
c) a little

426. She pretended that she agreed with me to
avoid … my feelings.
a) hurting
b) to hurt
c) hurt
427. Many fires could be … if new safety
standards were introduced.
a) protected
b) excluded
c) prevented

428. My watch stopped so I had no way of knowing the right … .
a) moment
b) time
c) hour

429. He came … an unknown poem while he was searching for something
else.
a) round
b) across
c) off

430. I couldn't beat him at chess; I'm just not in his … .
a) class
b) type
c) set

431. Too much exercise can be harmful but walking is good … you.
a) by
b) with
c) for

432. I find it difficult to talk to her because we have so … in common.
a) few
b) less
c) little

433. His attitude … his parents is very disrespectful.
a) as far as
b) towards
c) as for

434. Surely Anna is not going to drive, … she?
a) does

b) will
c) is

435. You … pay for this. It's free.
a) shouldn't
b) mustn't
c) don't have to

436. A child learns a language best … .
a) when being brought up to it
b) by being brought up to it

c) while being brought into it

437. Urgent discussions will continue … .
a) behind the scenes
b) behind the curtain
c) behind the bars

438. Our house is nothing out of the … .
a) normal
b) usual
c) ordinary

439. "A ladies' man" means:
a) a man most women fall for
b) a man who dresses up like a woman
c) a man who enjoys the company of women

440. The manager warned Kate that the laziness and … could result in her
dismissal.
a) procrastination
b) ambition
c) fortitude

441. The butcher cut some steak and … it up.
a) closed
b) wrapped
c) wound

442. The man … to take a breath test after the incident.
a) denied
b) objected
c) refused

443. I do my best to practise every day … it is difficult sometimes.
a) although
b) also
c) even

444. His arm was so … injured that he couldn't play anymore.
a) deeply
b) badly
c) hardly

445. His home is a … between a palace and a hotel.
a) union
b) link

c) cross

446. The woman … case was described in the article never fully recovered.
a) what
b) whom
c) whose

447. I … put my money there if I didn't consider it was safe.
a) didn't
b) wouldn't
c) hadn't

448. Driving in this city is supposed to be confusing but I didn't find it at … difficult.
a) all
b) once
c) least

449. I enjoy … but don't like jogging.
a) to swim
b) in swim
c) swimming

450. Would you … the kettle on for some coffee?
a) set
b) put
c) have

451. I suggest … the "meal of the day" rather than fish.
a) to have

b) we have
c) for us having

452. Her father won't … to my marrying Olivia.
a) agree
b) allow
c) approve

453. It was way to hot. I couldn't … it any longer.
a) carry
b) hold
c) stand

454. They had always liked the sea … they moved to the Coast.

a) so
b) since
c) such

455. Just keep .. on him, will you?
a) a look
b) an eye
c) a care

456. By the time you receive this message, I … for China.
a) will leave
b) have left
c) will have left

457. You can depend … me.
a) in
b) of
c) on

458. I invested a lot of money … residential buildings.
a) in
b) for
c) at

459. She is trying to lose weight by … sweets.
a) cutting down at
b) stopping down at
c) cutting down on

460. The terrorist tried to persuade the hostage that he was neither … nor … . He was just interested in calling attention to his cause.
a) impeccable/sincere
b) antagonistic/vindictive
c) recalcitrant/clandestine

461. The professor was surprised that her English was so … .
a) liquid
b) definite
c) fluent

462. I went to … some pictures by a renowned painter.
a) watch
b) look at
c) see to

463. If it … fine, she shall go out.
a) was
b) were
c) is
464. The idea of a balanced diet is difficult to …
in this group.
a) put across
b) take in
c) make over
465. There was a small room into … we all
gathered.
a) where
b) that
c) which
466. You … go to dentist's.
a) rather
b) ought to
c) better
467. His speech was interesting at first, but it
was … long.
a) so much
b) far too
c) too much
468. The soldier has been on … for twenty-four
hours without a break.
a) work

b) job
c) duty
469. When she braked on the icy road, the car
… .
a) slid
b) slipped
c) skidded
470. This is the … building in the city.
a) oldest
b) elder
c) elderly
471. You must put your name on this side and
then sign on the … side.
a) other
b) under
c) back

472. I will always … our wonderful holidays.
a) reflect
b) remind
c) remember
473. The Prime Minister … his intention to
retire.
a) told
b) announced
c) informed
474. As the child walked through the fields, he
heard sheep … .
a) braying
b) bleating
c) crying
475. I'm afraid I can't comment … your project
yet.
a) about
b) with
c) on
476. Steve was employed … a factory in 2010.
a) in
b) to
c) by

477. It was such a good weather that I decided
to go … .
a) fish
b) fishing
c) to fishing
478. I think she … you my regards when you
met two days ago.
a) gave
b) has given
c) give
479. Not … did she refuse to speak to me, but
she also blamed me for
failing.
a) even
b) at all
c) only
480. "To come through flying colours" means:
a) to succeed in one's study
b) to accomplish something with great success

c) to be understood loud and clear

481. I hope she is … to buy some milk.

a) proposed

b) suggested

c) remembered

482. If I were you, I … that gaming PC.

a) would buy

b) will buy

c) am buying

483. The vet decided that he had to operate …
the dog.

a) with

b) on

c) at

484. I … like to apologize.

a) could

b) must

c) would

485. Many accidents in the home could be … by
taking simple safety
measures.

a) protected

b) avoided

c) preserved

Set 5

486. Try to remember … bring your debit card.

a) me to

b) yourself to

c) to

487. The bride looked … in her dress.

a) beauty

b) lovely

c) handsome

488. We didn't leave for the station until the
very … moment.

a) late

b) least

c) last

489. When are you going to give back that book
you … me?

a) owe

b) debt

c) lend

490. The poor man was … by a gang last month.

a) murdered

b) destroyed

c) slaughter

491. Each … of the family had to do the
washing up.

a) person

b) member

c) individual

492. The woman performs beautifully … the
piano.

a) in

b) from

c) on

493. The boy comes … drawing lessons four
times a week.

a) to

b) for

c) at

494. She … a coloured thread round her finger
so as not to forget about the
meeting.

a) rang

b) wound

c) curved

495. You have a new baby?! …!

a) What wonderful news

b) What a wonderful news

c) How wonderful news

496. If my diploma … last week, I would have
been able to come sooner.

a) are found

b) were found

c) had been found

497. Old people do not take kindly to having
their daily … upset.

a) routine

b) habit

c) custom

498. You were warned never … with those members.

a) to assign

b) to assume

c) to associate

499. If your company wants to attract workers it must … the wages.

a) spread

b) raise

c) rise

500. This computer package is totally … for our need.

a) unsuitable

b) undeniable

c) unspeakable

501. Some people think it is … to use little-known words.

a) clever

b) skilled

c) sensitive

502. He decided to … from the committee.

a) cancel

b) resign

c) prevent

503. Be here at nine o'clock without … .

a) fault

b) late

c) fail

504. The children were … by the cartoons.

a) fascinated

b) fascinating

c) fascination

505. The murderer … escape from the prison.

a) could

b) managed to

c) succeeded in

506. A witness … now been found.

a) was

b) had

c) has

507. She couldn't tell the truth. She had to … a story.

a) invent

b) manage

c) combine

508. She woke up crying because she had … a nightmare.

a) seen

b) dreamt

c) had

509. I hope to get an answer to my final letter by … of post.

a) round

b) return

c) back

510. Didn't it ever … to you that you would be caught?

a) occur

b) enter

c) strike

511. I started early … to avoid the worst of the traffic.

a) so that

b) in so far

c) in order

512. The children threw snowballs at … on their way.

a) themselves

b) each other

c) their own

513. Don't be so sure … yourself.

a) of

b) with

c) on

514. My grandmother buys eggs … the dozen.

a) to

b) for

c) by

515. She's entitled … a pension, but she doesn't want to retire.

a) to

b) on

c) in
516. Before you run … other people, you should consider your own faults.
a) over
b) up
c) down
517. The child won't go to sleep … we leave a light on.
a) except
b) unless
c) but
518. The effectiveness of his work relies … the use of advanced technologies.
a) on
b) by
c) of
519. The minority are suing the government for the return of their … lands.
a) antique

b) ancestral
c) inherited
520. Some species are on the … of becoming extinct.
a) edge
b) side
c) verge
521. One … of my job is that it is near where I live.
a) advantage
b) pleasure
c) preference
522. The little child loved … the old castle.
a) hunting
b) detecting
c) exploring
523. This is a photo of the university I … when I lived in Hamburg.
a) used
b) attended
c) joined
524. It's the first time … here.

a) I have been
b) I was
c) I am coming
525. Many accidents in this town are caused by … driving.
a) harmful
b) careful
c) careless
526. I was delighted when I … to sell my car so quickly.
a) managed
b) could
c) risked
527. It sounds … the situation isn't about to improve.
a) how
b) as if
c) so that

528. This patient … quickly after his illness.
a) recovered
b) covered
c) discovered
529. Caring for her cousin is a … burden for her.
a) sour
b) bitter
c) heavy
530. The manager made a wonderful … .
a) message
b) talk
c) speech
531. There is a fault at our latest TV station. Please don't … your TV set.
a) repair
b) adjust
c) switch
532. The man … going by plane instead of car.
a) suggested
b) agreed
c) convinced
533. Please concentrate … your tasks!
a) with

b) to

c) on

534. Many men do not approve … blood-sports.

a) for

b) of

c) with

535. You must encourage Mary … her efforts.

a) in

b) at

c) with

536. The ball … two or three times before disappearing.

a) leapt

b) bounced

c) hopped

537. It's … helping that man. He will die anyway.

a) good

b) no good

c) not good

538. Would you agree that a man pays less attention … than a woman does?

a) to dress

b) on dress

c) to the dress

539. Our institution can give you the … number of refugees.

a) unclear

b) suggestive

c) approximate

540. As drunk as … . This phrase refers to someone very drunk.

a) a fish

b) a lord

c) a barrel

541. How … you manage to get there so fast?

a) used

b) had

c) did

542. The touristic guide walked so … that most of the people could not keep up with him.

a) fast

b) quick

c) rapid

543. Membership of the club, … costs $12,000 a year, is only open to women.

a) what

b) that

c) which

544. The boy swore that he would take … his family's killer.

a) revenge in

b) revenge on

c) revenge at

545. … she wasn't feeling very well, she went to visit her parents as usual.

a) Still

b) Although

c) However

546. That guy has a dishonest … in his character.

a) stripe

b) strip

c) streak

547. Having looked the place …, the strange man went away.

a) down

b) out

c) over

548. I'm selling the building … of the summer.

a) at the end

b) in the end

c) on the end

549. She was complaining … a headache this morning.

a) at

b) from

c) of

550. You need to hurry because the … train leaves in five minutes.

a) latter

b) last

c) latest

551. I am not used … spoken to in such a manner.
a) for being
b) to being
c) to be

552. There was a small house standing … hundreds of palm trees near the beach.
a) in
b) among
c) between

553. As the team were … at the end of the game, he lost the bet.
a) equal
b) fair
c) correct

554. These little stores are always … of people at Christmas time.
a) stuffed
b) busy
c) crowded

555. Their request … me completely by surprise.
a) left
b) made
c) took

556. I have … why the Browns went to live in that country.
a) puzzled
b) surprised
c) wondered

557. You have to be patient … him.
a) for
b) with
c) about

558. Most women never … with violent crimes.
a) get into contact
b) come into contact
c) get in touch

559. I don't think I … this game before.
a) have played

b) will play
c) would play

560. "A City man" refers to:
a) any man with a higher education
b) a man who works in a city, which is a financial power of an area
c) someone who is constantly showing off

561. Is there a bank where I can … these pounds for euros?
a) turn

b) alter
c) exchange

562. The officer said that he saw no … between the murders.
a) joint
b) connection
c) join

563. Drinking is a bad habit, which many people find difficult to … .
a) beat
b) cough
c) break

564. Would you … passing this magazine to him?
a) mind
b) agree
c) want

565. There's … to be frightened of the cat.
a) a fear
b) no need
c) no fear

566. Her boyfriend won't … her drive his car.
a) allow
b) leave
c) let

567. The competitors in the rally had to follow the … laid down by the sponsors.
a) direct
b) route
c) address

568. If only I …play the piano as well as you!

a) might
b) would
c) could
569. It's a great … that the exhibition was cancelled.
a) sorrow
b) sadness
c) pity

570. On our … to Madrid, the car broke down.
a) way
b) road
c) voyage
571. She has adopted two orphans … her own children.
a) except
b) besides
c) in place of
572. I cannot understand how you put … this residential area.
a) out
b) by
c) up with
573. You will have to take things … .
a) like you find them
b) as you find them
c) so as you find them
574. We … to the concert, but we didn't make it.
a) were to have gone
b) would go
c) were gone
575. No one … she was.
a) could be quicker than
b) can be as quick as
c) could be so quick as
576. This computer is cheap, but that one is … .
a) cheaper yet
b) more cheaper
c) even cheaper
577. If the line is busy, don't wait and … .
a) hang on
b) hang up

c) hang down
578. If they … to that event, they would certainly have decided to attend it.
a) will be invited
b) had been invited
c) were invited
579. If I saw Olive, I … her to my party.
a) invite
b) will invite
c) would invite
580. I was very … not to pass the message further.
a) cajoled
b) tempted
c) elicited
581. After the party the dog was allowed to finish off the … sandwiches.
a) left
b) leaving
c) remaining
582. I would much … a reply by the end of the week.
a) appreciate
b) require
c) value
583. When she heard the joke, she burst into loud … .
a) smiles
b) laughter
c) enjoyment
584. I couldn't get used to … to work so early.
a) go
b) going
c) be going
585. … amount of money can buy a true friend.
a) No
b) Never
c) None
586. They should be spending money on a house … than on a car.
a) other
b) better

c) rather

587. I was very … of myself for forgetting that.
a) disgraced
b) ashamed
c) shocked
588. Mary earns a great … of money.
a) quantity
b) level
c) deal
589. He is an expert … coronaviruses.
a) about
b) on
c) in
590. They look exactly the … .
a) alike
b) identical
c) same
591. There was no need to be uneasy … the results.
a) for
b) about
c) on
592. It's impossible to prevent the boys … quarrelling with each other.
a) to
b) in
c) from
593. This bike is inferior … the one I bought last year.
a) to
b) at
c) by
594. Tom plays … the school team.
a) by
b) in
c) on
595. The teacher despairs … ever teaching him anything.
a) of

b) in
c) on

596. Our family is fortunate in having sufficient supplies … the winter.
a) for
b) on
c) to
597. The old man was found guilty … many crimes.
a) from
b) for
c) of
598. … Sam, he can't go alone.
a) As if
b) As for
c) As far as
599. I know nothing about that battle. It was … .
a) behind the times
b) as the same time
c) before my time
600. Many jobs in this area can be directly … to tourism.
a) attributed
b) attracted
c) dedicated
601. When the director went to China on business his … took over all his duties.
a) officer
b) deputy
c) caretaker
602. She saw the plane crash when its engines … .
a) failed
b) struck
c) held
603. You are going to come to the meeting, …?
a) will you
b) do you
c) aren't you

604. You will not finish that project by tomorrow unless you … some help.
a) get
b) would get

c) will get

605. It's difficult to pay my bills when prices keep … .
a) rising
b) gaining
c) raising

606. After the death of her father, she was brought … by her uncle.
a) round
b) about
c) up

607. Why did the police suspect you? It doesn't make … to me.
a) right
b) sense
c) truth

608. When they heard that their children had crossed the road without
looking, they told them they … do it again.
a) mustn't
b) needn't
c) didn't need to

609. He went to Germany hoping to find a teaching … .
a) work
b) occupation
c) post

610. I can't … what they are doing; it's way too dark down there.
a) look into
b) make out
c) see through

611. This country has … good transport.
a) the
b) a
c) very

612. I'd like you to meet a very good friend of …, Dave.
a) me

b) my
c) mine

613. We travelled to Australia by the most … route.
a) direct
b) unique
c) easy

614. This film is based … a novel.
a) of
b) on
c) in

615. I should be grateful … any advice you can give regarding this
situation.
a) for
b) about
c) with

616. I was shocked … her indifference!
a) on
b) with
c) at

Set 6

617. The manager has just gone on her … leave. She gets three weeks'
holiday a year.
a) regular
b) annual
c) regular

618. He have … this minute left for the city centre.
a) ever
b) already
c) just

619. To my …, a pandemic is more dangerous than nuclear arms.
a) mind
b) view
c) disbelief

620. They are always … with each other about investments.
a) shouting

b) arguing

c) annoying

621. I took that faulty laptop back to the shop where I'd bought it and asked
the … if they would change it for me.

a) clerk

b) official

c) assistant

622. I … to the cinema last night. I'm so tired now.

a) had not to go

b) shouldn't have gone

c) haven't had to go

623. You will spend at least one year working in this company … you can
find out how things operate here.

a) so that

b) so as to

c) because

624. I can … with most things but I cannot stand lies.

a) put aside

b) put up

c) put off

625. I think she is … her time looking for a job here.

a) losing

b) wasting

c) missing

626. It is a very good idea to be … dressed when you have a business
meeting.

a) finely

b) smartly

c) boldly

627. I was pleased to see how … he looked after his recent COVID-19
illness.

a) well

b) pleasant

c) nice

628. Let's … across this field instead of going by the road.

a) set

b) come

c) cut

629. Tell me … about your holiday in Spain.

a) every

b) much

c) all

630. It's fairly rude to interrupt when someone is … .

a) talking

b) saying

c) discussing

631. I didn't enjoy the event. No, and … .

a) neither we did

b) we didn't either

c) so didn't we

632. … of the week, I hope I shall have lost another kilo.

a) By the end

b) At the end

c) To the end

633. I reasoned … her, but she would not listen to me.

a) to

b) for

c) with

634. She is responding … treatment and will be cured.

a) on

b) for

c) to

635. Nothing will prevent me … succeeding.

a) on

b) from

c) in

636. Jennifer criticised everything and even ran … his friends.

a) up

b) down

c) into

637. Why did you have … his last tutorial?

a) such difficulties to follow

b) such a difficulty to follow

c) such difficulty in following

638. I was sitting in a famous café … afternoon when I saw her.

a) one

b) in

c) the

639. The … question in this case is whether she was there or not.

a) crucial

b) valuable

c) supreme

640. He's the best employee I've ever had. I couldn't … for a better one.

a) abide

b) average

c) ask

641. You are not allowed … in this room.

a) smoke

b) smoking

c) to smoke

642. I think you'd better … before the manager returns.

a) be gone

b) be going

c) being gone

643. "I … you all", she said, as she left.

a) am hating

b) can hate

c) hate

644. I'm sorry. It's all my …!

a) guilt

b) fault

c) wrong

645. I chose these because they are my … shade of blue.

a) popular

b) favourite

c) fancy

646. I wonder … like to travel by boat.

a) what it is

b) how it is

c) what is it

647. Two other … in their report are worth mentioning.

a) effects

b) points

c) notices

648. Many soldiers were … wounded in the war. They needed a lot of help.

a) hardly

b) seriously

c) utterly

649. She's a luck person. She always seems to fall on her … .

a) ankles

b) legs

c) feet

650. … experience of working in a factory is required.

a) Previous

b) First

c) Initial

651. For a short time after the car crash, I suffered from constant … in my back.

a) hurt

b) pain

c) ache

652. An enormous … of rubbish had built up here.

a) pile

b) hill

c) tower

653. Children can be instructed … swimming at a very early age.

a) with

b) for

c) in

654. Marry will come … home late. Don't wait for her.

a) to

b) into

c) back

655. I was instructed … driving once upon a time.
a) in
b) about
c) at

656. How can you agree … such an idea?
a) with
b) at
c) by

657. It was … to meet you. That's what she said to me.
a) pleasure
b) a pleasure
c) some pleasure

658. Only by shouting loudly … a taxi.
a) she got
b) she's got
c) did she get

659. The lights … out and I was left in the darkness.
a) turned
b) went
c) gave

660. For this meal to be a real success, you … cook the meat for at least three hours.
a) need
b) ought
c) must

661. It is logical that when factories are … workers tend to lose their jobs.
a) automatic
b) automation
c) automated

662. They are not used … supper so late.
a) to having
b) of having
c) to have

663. Be careful; she has her eyes … you.
a) for
b) at
c) on

664. In spite of the anesthetic, I was fully … during the operation.
a) awake
b) sensitive
c) conscious

665. Today a man was … down the street by my dog.
a) chased
b) hunted
c) sped

666. I don't … to see her again until next month.
a) think
b) expect
c) wait

667. Some drivers, after …, annoy their fellows.
a) passing by
b) taking over
c) overtaking

668. I had … news of what she was doing in London.
a) several
b) little
c) few

669. Now that he is retired, he enjoys … more time watching documentaries.
a) spending
b) to take
c) taking

670. His debt now amounts … $10,000.
a) in

b) with
c) to

671. You demand too much of them; they are not really equal … the project.
a) for
b) to
c) with

672. The student is still dependent … his parents.

a) on
b) from
c) with

673. Will you have … to tell your manager about it?
a) some nerves
b) some nerve
c) the nerve

674. Boys and girls … enjoyed the show.
a) both
b) either
c) alike

675. The reconstruction of the city is now … .
a) well under way
b) well in the way
c) through the way

676. The production goes well now, although there were some … .
a) last straws
b) teething troubles
c) starting problems

677. If I could understand this alphabet, I … the article.
a) read
b) will read
c) would read

678. Please … and see me some time – you are welcome.
a) come to
b) come away
c) come around

679. I could … panic in her voice.
a) desist
b) detect
c) detest

680. Thousands of tourists use the … of footpaths across these hills.
a) network
b) grid
c) circuit

681. The professors … with coronavirus infection one after the other.

a) went down
b) went off
c) went under

682. He agreed to give me $100, … the $300 he had already lent me.
a) extra to
b) surplus to
c) in addition to

683. What do you usually … for delivering things?
a) demand
b) charge
c) cost

684. We chose some attractive … paper for the present.
a) covering
b) wrapping
c) packing

685. It was a beautiful cloth … from velvet.
a) worn
b) threaded
c) woven

686. We have … of time to catch the flight.
a) enough
b) plenty
c) great deal

687. She put the letters into the wrong envelopes … mistake.
a) on

b) with
c) by

688. Mike seems confident but you … never judge by appearances.
a) might
b) should
c) could

689. I couldn't go fishing because it began to … with rain.
a) flow
b) drench
c) pour

690. They … for the same job.

a) chose
b) referred
c) applied
691. The plane was … for over two hours because of fog.
a) delayed
b) landed
c) cancelled
692. She has to be careful which soap she uses, because her skin is … .
a) sensible
b) senseless
c) sensitive
693. The local authorities want people to set … their own businesses.
a) off
b) up
c) in
694. She is quite intelligent but she … common sense.
a) wants
b) fails
c) lacks
695. I wonder who drank all the wine. It … have been Mike because he was out all day.
a) can't
b) could
c) must

696. They are opposed … giving people large pay rises.
a) for
b) to
c) against
697. I will show you the document if I … it.
a) could find
b) will find
c) find
698. Being exhausted, he sent a request asking that his colleagues … their meeting for one hour.
a) defray

b) defer
c) commence
699. The reporter gave a dramatic … of his adventures.
a) tale
b) saga
c) account
700. Some people are camping for the … of rare species hunting.
a) extinction
b) abolition
c) annihilation
701. I am … in information about this laptop.
a) interested
b) bored
c) concerned
702. They say we're likely to have a … winter.
a) calm
b) smooth
c) mild
703. Do you think Sarah and Tom marry …?
a) lastly
b) at last
c) in the end
704. You should … a lawyer before you sign that contract.
a) check
 b) consult
c) counsel
705. "You can take a horse to water, but you can't … it drink!"
a) make   b) compel   c) save

Set 7

706. The old man is a little bit … in his right ear.
a) disabled
b) deaf
c) dead

707. Some explorers did not survive the terrible … across the mountains.
a) journey
b) step
c) travel
708. Heavy snowfalls have … all flights.
a) omitted
b) delayed
c) postponed
709. The rainstorms … more than three days.
a) went
b) took
c) lasted
710. There will be a … interval for snacks.
a) small
b) short
c) light
711. The play was very long, but there were three … .
a) rests
b) intervals
c) gaps
712. The jewels were … a lot of money.
a) cost
b) valued
c) worth

713. They had a plan to trick me, but I didn't fall … it.
a) for
b) to
c) at
714. It is unreasonable to demand this … Mary.
a) in
b) at
c) of
715. It took me a long time to get rid … the infection.
a) of
b) against
c) from
716. They differ … each other so much.
a) of

b) with
c) from
717. There is little … in this company.
a) hanging around
b) to hang around
c) hung around
718. I would let her go, if I … all about this mission.
a) know
b) have known
c) knew
719. They were … for smuggling perfumes into the country.
a) judged
b) warned
c) arrested
720. They didn't believe his theory because it didn't seem at all … .
a) feasible
b) plausible
c) creditable
721. … you leave for the airport, you'll miss the flight.
a) Unless

b) However
c) When
722. I haven't met her, but I did once … across her boyfriend.
a) look
b) go
c) come
723. She … her next appointment at the dentist's.
a) erased
b) cancelled
c) wiped
724. Because of the earthquake, the windows … in their frames.
a) rattled
b) slapped
c) shocked

725. I would … go by air than spend two days travelling by car.
a) prefer
b) better
c) rather

726. It's all over between them: she's walked … on him.
a) off
b) away
c) out

727. Our best player got infected and won't be … to play tomorrow.
a) adequate
b) fit
c) proper

728. Sarah spoke so fast I couldn't understand … she was talking about.
a) what
b) which
c) how

729. Mr. Smith is free … you now.
a) see
b) will see
c) to see

730. Everyone felt … for Mr. Brown when he lost his management position.
a) discontent
b) sorry
c) unhappy

731. What … will this decision have on the future of this company?
a) effect
b) result
c) answer

732. This year the trees were … two weeks earlier than usual.
a) in full cry
b) in full bloom
c) at full blast

733. During the last meeting everyone shared … his happiness.
a) in

b) against
c) at

734. The professional climber failed … his attempt.
a) with
b) at
c) in

735. I tried to reason … her, but she was rude to me.
a) on
b) with
c) for

736. Are you aware … the difficulties that lie ahead?
a) by
b) on
c) of

737. It's just an illusion. He's not different … anyone else.
a) for
b) from
c) on

738. Dave usually goes there … him.
a) with
b) to
c) at

739. Alexia worships the sun and … she spends her holidays in Greece.
a) yet
b) however
c) accordingly

740. I can't come. I'm tied … at the office.
a) in
b) up
c) down

741. Guests wore … they liked to the party.
a) everything
b) anything
c) nothing

742. The pilot drives so quickly that I am afraid that one day he will … someone.

a) crash down

b) turn over

c) knock down

743. Don't worry. This dog is perfectly … .

a) harmless

b) harmful

c) tame

744. One of the main advantages … the new operating platform is that it is

very simple to use.

a) for

b) of

c) on

745. You'd better set off twenty minutes early … there is traffic.

a) in case

b) so that

c) as if

746. When I saw Olivia's reaction, I regretted … told her.

a) to have

b) to having

c) having

747. The shirt I was wearing that day was dirty, but I don't think anyone …

.

a) watched

b) noticed

c) remarked

748. This is the oldest house … the village.

a) in

b) by

c) to

749. Jane was singing an old rock song, a favourite of … .

a) her

b) herself

c) hers

750. So … people came to the meeting that they had to cancel it.

a) a few

b) few

c) little

751. Scientists are still looking for a cure … COVID-19.

a) for

b) against

c) to

752. Put the salt in the water and let it … before adding anything else.

a) melt

b) dissolve

c) soften

753. It's too hot for you … this parcel.

a) digging

b) for digging

c) to dig

754. He told Steve … for borrowing his laptop without permission.

a) on

b) out

c) off

755. In this company, if you interfere … other people's affairs, you will

regret it.

a) with

b) to

c) about

756. Are you at least partially aware of the difficulties that lie ahead …

you?

a) for

b) of

c) to

757. I left my office after I … the report.

a) had written

b) have written

c) should have written

758. Her medical doctor made her … in bed for two weeks.

a) to stay

b) staying

c) stay

759. As quick as … . This phrase means very quick.
a) cats
b) fire
c) lightning

760. The officers haven't had time to complete the investigation, but they
have concluded … that he committed suicide.
a) tentatively
b) tenuously
c) temporally

761. I'm going to buy a new car; I'm tired … this one.
a) of
b) in
c) with

762. … a personal computer can help you work much faster.
a) To have
b) In having
c) Having

763. I … be delighted to show you the way.
a) might
b) ought to
c) would

764. … the weather, the match went ahead.
a) Owing to
b) In spite of
c) However

765. Melania rang to make an early … at the hairdresser's.
a) order
b) appointment
c) date

766. Adrian was the … in his family.
a) lowest
b) littlest
c) shortest

767. Could you buy a cake please … they come this afternoon?
a) if only
b) in case

c) on account of

768. One … of old public transport is its unreliability.
a) disorder
b) dislike
c) disadvantage

769. Did you know that she is … a baby?
a) expecting
b) hoping
c) waiting

770. The main … to progress is not technical but political.
a) clash
b) obstacle
c) prevention

771. The best rooms in this hotel … the bay.
a) regard

b) overlook
c) view

772. All dogs … be kept on a lead in public.
a) must
b) ought
c) need

773. You should separate the eggs and then beat with a … .
a) whip
b) wick
c) whisk

774. The man was … to steal the laptop when he saw it on the table.
a) dragged
b) tempted
c) brought

775. My parents … me to learn English when I was a child.
a) let
b) heard
c) persuaded

776. I am accustomed … bad weather.
a) to
b) of
c) from

777. She was afraid … mentioning it to her husband.
a) in
b) at
c) of
778. I warned them … the danger.
a) at
b) of
c) in
779. Gold is feared … in price this week.
a) to go up
b) going up
c) to be going up

780. I will ask Jane to come if I … her.
a) saw
b) will see
c) see
781. In the jar there was a … which looked like jam.
a) material
b) solid
c) substance
782. Because his presentation was so confusing, … people understood it.
a) clever
b) few
c) less
783. I am … her to arrive at any moment.
a) expecting
b) waiting
c) hoping
784. You … worry about the bill – I've already paid it.
a) daren't
b) might not
c) needn't
785. I've made an appointment for 11 o'clock. Is that … for you?
a) fit
b) convenient
c) right
786. You look … you've seen a ghost!
a) so that
b) that
c) as if
787. You … blame yourself. It wasn't your fault.
a) daren't
b) won't
c) mustn't
788. I'm … that I didn't pass the examination.
a) deceived

b) despaired
c) disappointed
789. This magazine has … interesting article on space travel.
a) quite an
b) a partly
c) nearly an
790. Your sister is much taller … you.
a) how
b) than
c) from
791. They always quarrel about coffee; she likes it strong, but he wants it …
.
a) small
b) feeble
c) weak
792. Getting divorced was a … decision for us.
a) firm
b) hard
c) large
793. Mr. Smith was … in a road accident.
a) damaged
b) wronged
c) injured
794. I expected her at eight but she finally … at midnight.
a) came to
b) turned up
c) came off
795. Buses into town run … ten minutes or so.
a) each

b) all
c) every
796. Can you make … what she has written there?
a) for
b) out
c) up for

797. I can't say what his name is though it is … .
a) on the tip of my tongue
b) on top of my tongue
c) on my tongue's tip
798. Whether or not to abolish corporal punishment is still … in political circles.
a) proposal of contention
b) a bone of contention
c) bone of agreement
799. I … a nice watch two days ago.
a) was given
b) have been given
c) would give
800. As bold as … . This phrase means cheeky, impudent.
a) bones
b) a bear
c) brass
801. He was an … writer because he persuaded many people.
a) ordinary
b) influential
c) accurate
802. I … seeing Mary tomorrow so I will give her your message.
a) may be
b) shall be
c) could be
803. The temperature yesterday was about … for this season.
a) average
b) middle
c) moderate

804. Steven swims well and … does his sister.
a) also
b) even
c) so
805. The old man was very … for my help.
a) grateful

b) pleased
c) delighted
806. … it was raining she went out without a raincoat.
a) In spite
b) However
c) Although
807. Your progress will be … in three months' time.
a) valued
b) evaluated
c) counted
808. I don't know why she complains. She doesn't earn as … as I do.
a) less
b) few
c) little
809. The organization will not be … any new members.
a) taking up
b) taking off
c) taking on
810. She can make a delicious … out of almost anything.
a) food
b) meal
c) plate
811. From now on, everything will be … sailing, I hope.
a) plain
b) simple
c) pretty
812. She could hardly … such a generous offer.
a) turn for
b) turn off
c) turn down

813. Tom has made his money by developing a travel … .
a) shop
b) business
c) affair

814. Do you believe … all that nonsense? I honestly don't.
a) in
b) to
c) at

815. I'm not sure … the exact date.
a) with
b) of
c) for

816. She's not capable … bringing up this child.
a) of
b) on
c) for

817. Steven was born … .
a) without wedlock
b) out of a wedlock
c) out of wedlock

818. Although he has travelled extensively, he has never been … .
a) to the Antipodes
b) at Antipodes
c) to Antipodes

819. At that hour, the street was … as people were fast asleep in bed.
a) denuded
b) deserted
c) devastated

820. Artists struggle with the conflict between … their own talent and
knowledge that very few succeed.
a) faith in
b) neglect of
c) dissolution to

821. My house isn't difficult to find. It's … the high school.
a) against
b) beside

c) between

822. A lot of my friends have … smoking in the last year.
a) put off

b) given up
c) held back

823. Please tell me … there is anything special that you would like to eat.
a) which
b) so
c) if

824. I'm making you responsible for this report. Please see … it that it is
finished on time.
a) for
b) into
c) to

825. Olivia suggested … to the cinema together.
a) that we should go
b) us to go
c) we are going

826. It will be mostly cloudy, with … of rain in the west.
a) bursts
b) outbreaks
c) times

827. I … of people who smoke.
a) dislike
b) distrust
c) disapprove

828. Jane bought a new … for the party.
a) dress   b) clothes   c) vest

Set 8

829. When the organization got a new computer, we had to … a
programming course.
a) do
b) make
c) study

830. This history lesson seemed to go … .
a) over and over

b) on and on
c) off and on
831. I know her by …, but I don't what her name is.
a) sight
b) heart
c) chance
832. The bus burst into … but the driver managed to escape.
a) heat
b) fire
c) flames
833. I know Jane is slow … understanding, but please be patient.
a) to
b) at
c) on
834. I'll be absent … class this week.
a) from
b) at
c) to
835. It gives me … to introduce her.
a) great pleasure
b) a great pleasure
c) much pleasures
836. They … in Germany for more than two years now.
a) were staying
b) are staying
c) have been staying
837. Look, I'm not drunk. I am as … as a judge.
a) calm
b) sober
c) clear
838. The working atmosphere has gone downhill. You have a lot to … for.
a) agree
b) abide
c) answer

839. That incident happened because of the … of the employees.
a) infallible
b) negligence
c) diligence
840. "A sore point" means:
a) a very dangerous crossroads
b) a matter that irritates or hurts when it is brought up
c) a blister on a foot
841. She likes to sit there and … what goes on below.
a) look
b) gaze
c) watch
842. Keep … the good work!
a) with
b) on
c) up
843. … he joined the army, Steve had never been abroad.
a) Until
b) Since
c) While
844. If you want to join our club, you must first … this application form.
a) do up
b) fill in
c) make up
845. I haven't got … furniture like theirs.
a) some
b) any
c) the
846. The librarian went to search for the book in a place … rare ones were kept.
a) where
b) there
c) that
847. A teacher must … children to be kind to each other.
a) let

b) force

c) encourage

848. You'll … a lot of time if you take the car.

a) spend

b) make

c) save

849. They took out a/an … to that newspaper.

a) inscription

b) subscription

c) conscription

850. The local authorities … increase taxes soon.

a) may

b) need

c) dare

851. The child hit the vase with his elbow and it … to the floor.

a) crashed

b) smashed

c) broke

852. I completely … with what has been said.

a) accept

b) agree

c) approve

853. She lost her homework and she … do it again.

a) ought

b) needs

c) has to

854. You are not … to smoke inside.

a) let

b) allowed

c) accepted

855. I believe … this town needs is a new shopping mall.

a) as

b) how

c) what

856. It's still not … that I am going to Madrid tomorrow.

a) certain

b) right

c) exact

857. Even though the old man was often cruel to his dog, it remained faithful … him.

a) for

b) in

c) to

858. You should encourage your daughter … her efforts.

a) to

b) for

c) in

859. The artists … our town by … .

a) have taken/by surprise

b) have taken/by storm

c) have brought/by storm

860. There is an increasing … to make films portraying love.

a) trend

b) surge

c) tradition

861. I felt sorry … him when he lost his job.

a) with

b) to

c) for

862. It was difficult for me to … what the recommendations I should make.

a) decide

b) realize

c) settle

863. The gorgeous lady walked to the … of the pool and jumped in.

a) extent

b) border

c) side

864. I thought she would like me to buy her a … brown bag.

a) black

b) French

c) new

865. The officer … me the way.

a) said

b) told
c) directed
866. Her boyfriend was sent to prison for … a bank.
a) stealing
b) robbing
c) lending
867. I'm going to stay here … she phones me.
a) for
b) when
c) until
868. You can trust what Daniel says. He's a very … person.
a) trustful
b) profitable
c) reliable
869. Don't worry. I still have one or two … up my sleeve.
a) tricks
b) defenses
c) jokes
870. The Prime Minister got up to … a short speech.
a) tell
b) make
c) hold
871. Mike was an … writer who persuaded many people.
a) influential
b) accurate
c) ordinary
872. If I hadn't done that, I think you … .
a) could die
b) might have died
c) may have died

873. People who live in big cities … to suffer from stress.
a) develop
b) tend
c) lean
874. She has provided … every emergency.
a) to

b) with
c) for
875. There was a note attached … the package.
a) to
b) with
c) on
876. They say Italian is a splendid language … .
a) for singing in
b) to sing in
c) for sing in
877. I saw him … the street.
a) crosses
b) to cross
c) cross
878. Although we have a large number of employees, each one receives … attention when needed.
a) only
b) individual
c) single
879. We negotiated for hours but we weren't able to … at an agreement.
a) agree
b) abide
c) arrive
880. The missing climber appeared at the mountain hut … and kicking.
a) alive
b) hale
c) safe
881. Sarah had had a special … with her aunt ever since her mother died.
a) sense

b) feeling
c) relationship
882. The little boy was so noisy that his mother told him not to be such a …
.
a) trouble
b) nuisance
c) worry

883. I took … football again at the beginning of this month.
a) up
b) with
c) by
884. Would you … the stamps on to the documents?
a) spit
b) suck
c) stick
885. The robber … everyone in the bank lie on the floor.
a) obliged
b) made
c) forced
886. There are … employees who always cause trouble.
a) these
b) that
c) some
887. I am late because my alarm clock … this morning. I'm sorry.
a) came on
b) went off
c) turned on
888. In spite of his protests, Steve … the athlete train two hours a day.
a) made
b) let
c) cause
889. The man was standing … of the diving board, showing off his muscles.
a) by the end
b) on the end
c) in the end

890. I mustn't stop … on this project for another two hours.
a) to work
b) working
c) to have work
891. Would you mind if I … the windows? It's hot in here.

a) did open
b) opened
c) were opening
892. The next time you see Jane, you … apologize.
a) ought to
b) need
c) dare to
893. If she's not back … midnight, I'm going to phone the police.
a) on
b) till
c) by
894. The man … his wife and children and left them to take care of themselves.
a) let
b) spoilt
c) abandoned
895. The customer … on complaining to the manager in person.
a) insisted
b) argued
c) demanded
896. They have a great … for that island because they spent their honeymoon there.
a) feeling
b) affection
c) connection
897. Like her, I hope … something better.
a) to
b) in
c) for

898. I would go to Rome if I … time to do it.
a) have
b) had
c) would have
899. I will play the piano but I'm a little … .
a) out of practice
b) out of use
c) out of turn

900. In this area coal is mined day … night.
a) into
b) after
c) and
901. I had to leave my family … when I went abroad to work.
a) at a loss
b) behind
c) out
902. The author had qualified as a medical doctor but later gave up the …
of medicine.
a) practice
b) procedure
c) prescription
903. It was … . I had to talk quickly to keep warm.
a) fresh
b) mild
c) cold
904. Her novel was more exciting … any she has written.
a) than
b) as
c) to
905. I'm having a party on Sunday. …?
a) Will you come
b) Don't you come
c) Need you come
906. The boy … his head, wondering how he could solve the equation.
a) shaved

b) screwed
c) scratched
907. She swatted some flies on the windows and … the glass.
a) crashed
b) smashed
c) cut
908. She received a e-mail this morning … her a place at university.
a) inviting

b) offering
c) proposing
909. The Browns spent so much money that they're … debt.
a) out of
b) with
c) in
910. … you open the windows, please?
a) Need
b) Will
c) May
911. Will you … what you said? It was rude!
a) take off
b) take up
c) take back
912. Stick this … on the parcel that says "fragile".
a) label
b) sign
c) advice
913. The manager … that the people he works with are very committed.
a) talks
b) says
c) tells
914. The girl learnt to ski on a slope that was not too … .
a) high
b) tall
c) steep

915. The trade … of the company if a bee.
a) mark
b) class
c) brand
916. You will not succeed … working harder on this project.
a) although
b) if
c) without
917. The old lady will never part … her precious possessions.
a) from

b) to

c) with

918. I am grateful … you.

a) to

b) for

c) by

919. They have to work hard for money while the fat … in the city make money doing very little.

a) pack

b) fish

c) cats

920. Youngsters need all the help and … when applying for jobs.

a) incentive

b) stimulation

c) encouragement

921. I'm sorry but I haven't got … change.

a) some

b) lots

c) any

922. Volkswagen is one of the most popular … of car in Germany.

a) makes

b) brands

c) marks

923. I must … shopping tomorrow.

a) to go

b) going

c) go

924. I can't see any … to this complicated problem.

a) result

b) solution

c) reason

925. Yesterday I came … a beautiful old car.

a) across

b) over

c) down

926. I can't find my book anywhere; it has simply … .

a) missed

b) lost

c) vanished

927. Scientists have discovered a close … between smoking and cancer.

a) action

b) connection

c) union

928. He came in quietly … not to wake the children.

a) so as

b) if so

c) as if

929. I decided to … a party to celebrate my promotion.

a) offer

b) give

c) make

930. I have no doubt … the innocence of the accused.

a) over

b) on

c) about

931. Everybody … me for the incident.

a) blamed

b) arrested

c) charged

932. Tomorrow the children are going to see the works … Van Gogh.

a) from

b) of

c) with

933. I consulted my lawyer … the matter and I shall continue.

a) for

b) to

c) on

Set 9

934. She didn't enjoy … at her aunt's.

a) to stay

b) staying
c) stayed
935. There are … when I have to drive for long
distances.
a) times
b) a long time
c) at times
936. … by the rejections of his articles, Daniel
… to submit his works to
other publishers.
a) Undaunted/continued
b) Elated/planned
c) Inspired/complied
937. When Mary heard the latest bad news, she
hit the … .
a) head
b) bend
c) roof
938. It has been suggested that environment is
the … factor in the incidence
of drug addiction.
a) logical
b) conclusive
c) predominant
939. If the door bell … she would rush to
answer it.
a) rings
b) rang
c) has rung

940. The five friends all … for the same job.
a) applied
b) referred
c) requested
941. My laptop is out of order, which is a … .
a) hurt
b) harm
c) nuisance
942. We decided to go ahead with the match …
the bad weather.
a) unless
b) in spite
c) despite

943. She kept the job … the manager had
threatened to sack her.
a) although
b) even
c) unless
944. It takes most people seven to ten days to …
from COVID-19.
a) cure
b) recover
c) prevent
945. The building has been left empty for five
years; it will be expensive to
… the damage that has been done.
a) fix
b) repair
c) mend
946. The children were … by the noise in the
forest.
a) afraid
b) feared
c) frightened
947. No, thanks. I'm trying to … weight.
a) lose
b) rid
c) throw
948. Is there … at all I can do to help you?
a) someone

b) anything
c) no one
949. I'll have to wait until the mechanic … .
a) will come
b) is coming
c) comes
950. … you improve this project, you won't
pass the exam.
a) When
b) Unless
c) If
951. We got up early this morning … pack the
car for the journey.
a) in order to
b) so that

c) in case

952. I … that a shame!

a) calling

b) might call

c) call

953. When there are people about a deer … for the shelter of the forest.

a) takes

b) makes

c) seeks

954. I am anxious about the … of the negotiations.

a) output

b) outlook

c) outcome

955. We have been corresponding … each other for some years.

a) with

b) to

c) by

956. When questioned about the missing report, he firmly … that he had

ever seen it.

a) defied

b) refused

c) denied

957. Have you ever been introduced to …?

a) royalty

b) the royalty

c) royalties

958. Mary's rung … . I must have said something wrong.

a) off

b) round

c) back

959. The officers set a … to catch them.

a) trap

b) plan

c) device

960. The rise in the flat prices … him to sell his for a large profit.

a) achieved

b) enabled

c) managed

961. She enjoyed the dessert so much that she accepted a second … .

a) load

b) pile

c) helping

962. The little boy put a … against the tree and climbed up.

a) scale

b) grade

c) ladder

963. This is one of the London's most … hotels.

a) well-off

b) luxurious

c) rich

964. Some truck drivers expect everyone else to get … their way.

a) away from

b) off

c) out of

965. It's … long time since I last saw you.

a) such a

b) so

c) too

966. The dentist told me to open my mouth … .

a) broad

b) greatly

c) wide

967. Tom left home more than two hours ago. He … be at the office by

now.

a) can

b) must

c) would

968. I … you wear the blue coat.

a) say

b) suggest

c) encourage

969. When I was in London I went on a few short day … to tourist sights.

a) travels

b) voyages

c) trips

970. The purple curtains began to … after some time in the sun.

a) fade

b) dissolve

c) melt

971. Our new colleague seems calm enough, but he has a very violent … .

a) mood

b) temper

c) stage

972. It's three years … I went to Cambridge.

a) for

b) last

c) since

973. They can only cure Mary … her illness if they operate on her.

a) of

b) on

c) in

974. I believe … taking my time to finish this project.

a) on

b) in

c) with

975. That man is often extremely rude … people.

a) for

b) with

c) to

976. You demand too much … him.

a) of

b) for

c) in

977. The branch gave … and the cat found itself suddenly on the ground.

a) in

b) way

c) back

978. Mira saw her little sister … after the dog.

a) run

b) ran

c) runs

979. If you … Harry, tell him to come and see me.

a) have met

b) meet

c) met

980. Our study … in March if we receive all feedback.

a) is published

b) published

c) will be published

981. I kept the door open by putting a … under it.

a) triangle

b) block

c) wedge

982. … from Sarah, all the employees said they would go.

a) Apart

b) Except

c) Only

983. This cloth … quite thin.

a) touches

b) feels

c) holds

984. The boy says he has got … in his stomach.

a) hurt

b) pains

c) suffering

985. The drivers are complaining that their fares are too … .

a) small

b) little

c) low

986. The terrorist … the pilot to change direction.

a) forced

b) demanded

c) made

987. As soon as the alarm rang everyone walked quickly downstairs, …

gathered in the car park.
a) while
b) then
c) before
988. She has a strong … to see her town again.
a) liking
b) feeling
c) desire
989. Don't … your drink on the table. Be careful!
a) spill
b) flood
c) flow
990. This wet weather has lasted for two weeks; … rained every single day.
a) there has
b) it has
c) there was

991. It is a long … from Berlin to Moscow.
a) tour
b) track
c) flight
992. Do you mind not …?
a) to smoke
b) smoke
c) smoking
993. We will have to … sales during the coming year.
a) expand
b) increase
c) extend
994. The meeting, … I was the guest of honour, was enjoyable.
a) by which
b) for which
c) at which
995. That's the woman … daughter I nearly kissed when I was young.
a) whose
b) whom
c) that

996. I am thankful … any advice you could give me.
a) about
b) on
c) for
997. We haven't accused him … anything.
a) by
b) of
c) to
998. The spy surrendered himself … the enemy.
a) in
b) with
c) to
999. This shows continues to … various audiences.
a) enthrall

b) bored
c) catching
1000. The … of supplies and equipment has hampered the progress of medical research for a cure.
a) scarcity
b) rationing
c) discontinuance
1001. In this country home ownership has … rapidly since 1990.
a) raised
b) grown
c) enlarged
1002. Unfortunately, nobody … that airplane crash.
a) lived
b) released
c) survived
1003. We were so late reaching the station that we … missed the train.
a) almost
b) already
c) soon
1004. The director didn't offer her the job because of her untidy … .
a) sight

b) presence

c) appearance

1005. You … have seen them yesterday. They're on holiday.

a) mustn't

b) can't

c) needn't

1006. The mansion has been built on the … of a lake.

a) border

b) edge

c) front

1007. Her performance was …; everyone was delighted.

a) faultless

b) unmarked

c) worthless

1008. Please … your bill before you leave the shop.

a) control

b) figure

c) check

1009. I can't even make … where the road is.

a) out

b) up

c) over

1010. I found the articles rather dull; I couldn't read it … .

a) by the end

b) to the end

c) on the end

1011. She has to work hard to keep the house … and tidy.

a) smooth

b) neat

c) plain

1012. How much have you borrowed … me already? Don't you think that's enough?

a) of

b) from

c) on

1013. This coat will protect you … the cold.

a) from

b) about

c) of

1014. Spies may have a number of … names and documents.

a) false

b) artificial

c) synthetic

Set 10

1015. They were … after working all day.

a) tired out

b) worn out

c) tired down

1016. If I had known about the problem, I … him to go away.

a) told

b) would tell

c) would have told

1017. You … better be careful not to miss the class.

a) would

b) had

c) should

1018. I hope you don't mind me … so late at night. It's urgent.

a) telephone

b) telephoning

c) to telephone

1019. As cunning as a … . This phrase means very clever, very smart.

a) a fox

b) a leopard

c) an owl

1020. Molecular biology is one of the most interesting scientific … .

a) divisions

b) disciplines

c) matters

1021. Take the bus and get … at Black Lake Road.
a) off
b) down
c) outside
1022. Tom's sister had a baby daughter yesterday and she is his first … .
a) cousin
b) relation
c) niece
1023. Will the company be able to … all their difficulties?
a) overcome
b) dismiss
c) defeat
1024. There was nothing … to eat in the refrigerator.
a) at last
b) at all
c) at least

1025. The professor was angry with them because they kept … talking.
a) up
b) up with
c) on
1026. After going to several interviews, she … to get a job.
a) managed
b) could
c) achieved
1027. If only he … told the police the truth in the first place.
a) has
b) would have
c) had
1028. A small … of students was waiting outside the class.
a) team
b) group
c) gang
1029. Many countries rely on rice as the … food.

a) capital
b) staple
c) winning
1030. Please take your place in the … .
a) queue
b) tail
c) file
1031. I like to sit … the river and fish.
a) beside
b) next
c) along
1032. The poor man fell … in front of a train.
a) in full
b) in full cry
c) full length
1033. Her professor brought her some books … art.
a) on

b) for
c) with
1034. I am thinking of looking … a new job.
a) to
b) for
c) after
1035. I've never been good … math.
a) with
b) at
c) in
1036. It's pointless … .
a) asking her for help
b) to ask help from her
c) to ask her of helping
1037. There is no need for you to shout … .
a) at your top voice
b) on top of your voice
c) at the top of your voice
1038. I … him about it for more than two weeks.
a) am asking
b) have been asking
c) asked
1039. They … their success to hard work.

a) attribute

b) aim

c) angle

1040. Prescribed treatments can … the pain but cannot … the patient.

a) palliate/cure

b) alleviate/infect

c) abate/affect

1041. When the police found my wallet, it was … .

a) vacant

b) empty

c) deserted

1042. It was a sad day when the company closed and the employees were all … .

a) paid back

b) paid up

c) paid off

1043. You will become ill … you stop working so hard.

a) until

b) unless

c) if

1044. The sooner we leave this place, the …!

a) preferable

b) better

c) ideal

1045. The weather seems to be … .

a) clearing up

b) setting up

c) wearing off

1046. After some time you get used to the people's … of life.

a) habit

b) custom

c) way

1047. I can no longer afford the cost of … two cars.

a) operating

b) running

c) managing

1048. A soldier has to learn to carry … orders as soon as they are given.

a) on

b) off

c) out

1049. Too many players refuse to … the referee's decisions.

a) accept

b) allow

c) agree

1050. It's not fair that I … always have to clean the table.

a) should

b) would

c) must

1051. She won't have any problems. She's a very self-… young lady.

a) reliable

b) confident

c) trusting

1052. This summer was so hot that the … in the woods dried up.

a) bath

b) bowl

c) pond

1053. It's over a year … I visited the medical doctor.

a) past

b) since

c) when

1054. There's an interesting pc game … in today's newspaper.

a) advertised

b) informed

c) issued

1055. The lessons usually start … 8 p.m.

a) with

b) on

c) at

1056. I though you said that you were … to be in Germany this month.

a) supposed

b) intended

c) assumed

1057. Motorway traffic was … after a terrible accident.

a) diverged

b) diverted

c) deflected

1058. She is referred to as a/an … housewife.

a) only

b) sole

c) mere

1059. I wish she … change her mind so often!

a) shouldn't

b) wouldn't

c) couldn't

1060. The famous woman lived a life thought to be … even by her contemporaries.

a) exorbitant

b) extraneous

c) extravagant

1061. When I was a child I wanted to … to play the guitar.

a) know

b) learn

c) discover

1062. I really can't make … what's happening here.

a) away

b) over

c) out

1063. Mary has put on so much weight that her clothes don't … her any more.

a) match

b) fit

c) suit

1064. It's amazing what his mother lets him … away with.

a) get

b) make

c) go

1065. Steve … to the hospital ten minutes before her birth.

a) was

b) got

c) arrived

1066. The man took the stress to write … the complete list for us.

a) out

b) through

c) off

1067. … the papers, the Prime Minister is to give a speech tomorrow.

a) Related to

b) Referring to

c) According to

1068. Clearing the weeds was a much harder … than they had imagined.

a) deed

b) service

c) task

1069. Be careful! It's a minor road and … in places.

a) bending

b) wandering

c) winding

1070. My application was … .

a) turned down

b) let down

c) put down

1071. I am fond of his novels. He is my … author.

a) favourite

b) likely

c) favoured

1072. She studied chemistry at university and … .

a) so did I

b) so I did

c) I did also

1073. Biting one's fingernails is a very bad … .

a) custom

b) habit

c) way
1074. You … be serious about that. I won't do it.
a) mustn't
b) might not
c) can't
1075. He is so keen … learning. He should be encouraged.
a) in

b) on
c) for
1076. Don't blame me … that! It's not my fault.
a) to
b) with
c) for
1077. I don't think she had … me about her problems.
a) tells
b) to tell
c) telling
1078. The judge shouted to counsel on both sides that he would … no
argument.
a) hear
b) brook
c) accept
1079. The professor was … out of his job after the scandal.
a) wiped
b) eased
c) wiped
1080. He was unsure that the speech was word … .
a) perfect
b) precise
c) accurate
1081. Mike often … about his expensive car.
a) praises
b) boasts
c) prides
1082. Have you heard? Steven has got married … Susan.

a) to
b) with
c) by
1083. The boy went to bed … very ill.
a) feels
b) having felt
c) feeling

1084. Could you … me fifty dollars? I'll pay you back next Friday.
a) lend
b) take
c) borrow
1085. We hope that one day a cure for cancer will … .
a) find
b) be found
c) been found
1086. We have much pleasure in … the invitation.
a) taking
b) accepting
c) thanking
1087. Tom is a … player. He practises for three hours every morning.
a) keen
b) excited
c) impatient
1088. I had a … that something terrible was going to happen.
a) sense
b) view
c) feeling
1089. If you're trying to lose weight, you should … off fats.
a) eat
b) keep
c) go
1090. Tom decided to … a priest instead of joining the army.
a) train for
b) study for
c) become

1091. Jennifer … drive to the station every day.
a) using to
b) used to
c) had used to
1092. … hard he tries, she never wins at tennis.
a) Wherever

b) Whatever
c) However
1093. When the little boy was hit on the head, he … consciousness.
a) lost
b) fell
c) dropped
1094. The kid got a bad mark because he had … a lot of mistakes in his homework.
a) done
b) committed
c) made
1095. The student who … in his exams was expelled.
a) cheated
b) tricked
c) deceived
1096. The racing car came round the corner … full speed.
a) for
b) at
c) to
1097. I dreamt … you last night.
a) on   b) in   c) of

Set 11

1098. He … .
a) set off to a stroll
b) set off on a stroll
c) set down to a stroll
1099. If I can't be back on time, she … her dinner alone.
a) has

b) will have
c) would have
1100. As black as … . This phrase means very dirty.
a) the Ace of Spades
b) ink
c) night

1101. I'm very … in this information.
a) concerned
b) interested
c) surprised
1102. Since his wife died, he has gone to … .
a) fragments
b) bits
c) pieces
1103. I hope that you have read the report and understand … it means.
a) what
b) how
c) that
1104. The crowd's … was amazing.
a) inactive
b) reaction
c) interacted
1105. Sarah met her husband … a computer dating agency.
a) out of
b) from
c) through
1106. As far as I'm …, it's all right to leave now.
a) regarded
b) consulted
c) concerned
1107. There was a serious … of cholera last year.
a) outbreak
b) fallout
c) overflow
1108. The … of the employees led to a series of troubles.
a) sending

b) dismissal
c) parting
1109. She struggled for a time before she … to free herself.
a) managed

b) achieved
c) enabled
1110. She tried to find a good excuse to … the awkward situation.
a) get over for
b) get away
c) get out of
1111. This meat isn't that good; you have to … it for a long time.
a) chew
b) bite
c) swallow
1112. I wear a seat-belt … I have an accident.
a) unless
b) if
c) in case
1113. It takes a while to … in a new house.
a) settle up
b) settle down
c) settle on
1114. More people … football than play it.
a) watch
b) look
c) stare
1115. The conductor told her to get off because she couldn't pay the … .
a) fee
b) fare
c) bill
1116. She is qualified … typing.
a) to
b) at
c) in
1117. We have to … museums and encourage legitimate investors.
a) protect
b) undermine

c) perpetuate

1118. Despite some bad reviews, his importance was not … .
a) diminished
b) distilled
c) embellished
1119. "A French window" means … .
a) a windows with no glass
b) a double glass door that opens on to a garden or balcony
c) a windows that turns out to be too small
1120. Our fortune was … at more than $2 million.
a) judged
b) guessed
c) estimated
1121. To my …, her illness proved not to be as serious as I had feared.
a) anxiety
b) eyes
c) relief
1122. You shouldn't let him treat you like that. You must stand … him.
a) up to
b) by
c) for
1123. This public clock is not as … as it should be.
a) true
b) accurate
c) strict
1124. You … stay at home for another day.
a) had better
b) can better
c) would better
1125. The two cars collided with … loud a crash it woke me.
a) so
b) very
c) such
1126. I … the stolen bike when the insurance money arrived.

a) misplaced

b) displaced

c) replaced

1127. I'm looking forward … you again.

a) to see

b) to seeing

c) seeing

1128. This is a friendly community and everyone … each other very well.

a) gets on with

b) gets up to

c) gets down to

1129. Parking …!

a) stopped

b) prohibited

c) denied

1130. It's a good thing to give at least a two week's … before you leave.

a) time

b) leave

c) notice

1131. More often … not, it rains here in autumn.

a) than

b) if

c) as

1132. Now they are the … of friends.

a) most

b) best

c) nearest

1133. If … I had done it when I had the chance!

a) just

b) then

c) only

1134. She kept the business … for as long as possible.

a) to go

b) going

c) go

1135. This employee is very good .. finding excuses.

a) for

b) in

c) at

1136. … any of these documentaries before?

a) Did you see

b) Have you seen

c) Will you see

1137. Would you mind … these plates a wipe?

a) making

b) giving

c) getting

1138. The lung transplant operation is … complicated.

a) broadly

b) slightly

c) extremely

1139. I … be grateful if you could let me have the details.

a) should

b) ought to

c) might

1140. Do you know … there?

a) whose

b) who's

c) whom

1141. He looks as if he … be her brother.

a) can

b) would

c) could

1142. The little girl is as … as a mouse.

a) quiet

b) small

c) slight

1143. After her absence, she found it difficult to … up with the rest.

a) take

b) catch

c) make

1144. I got to the theatre just … to see the actors entering.

a) in time

b) on time

c) at times

1145. This job … many visits to landlords.
a) concerns
b) offers
c) involves
1146. Do you … my turning the laptop on?
a) want
b) mind
c) object
1147. Jack was not pleased about … called an idiot.
a) was
b) being
c) to be
1148. A hot lemon drink is good … a cold.
a) for
b) with
c) to
1149. I heard a … at the door.
a) lean
b) hit
c) knock
1150. The hotel is … walking distance of the sea.
a) close
b) within
c) inside
1151. The main … of this drink are wine and orange juice.
a) parts
b) ingredients
c) components

1152. Our hands smell … honey soap.
a) of
b) with
c) by
1153. I'm sure she … on 16th February.
a) hasn't come
b) don't come
c) didn't come
1154. If I see John, I … to him.
a) talk
b) would talk

c) will talk
1155. If I get tickets, I … you up.
a) will ring
b) ring
c) could ring
1156. Kate did all the work … her own.
a) by
b) on
c) for
1157. The officers arrested the … criminal.
a) famous
b) renowned
c) notorious
1158. The left faction prospers … the right is losing ground.
a) while
b) until
c) whether
1159. The student took down … quantities of notes.
a) extended
b) detailed
c) copious
1160. Open plains are … of the geography of this country.
a) distinctive

b) specific
c) characteristic
1161. It is a good idea to see your medic for … .
a) a revision
b) a check-up
c) a control
1162. If I had known your address, I … to see you.
a) would come
b) would have come
c) came
1163. Steve has … you some flowers.
a) carried
b) lifted
c) brought
1164. She played an active … in politics.

a) part

b) scene

c) job

1165. Chip-making is a very … work.

a) skilled

b) trained

c) educated

1166. Mary … him of wanting to marry her just for money.

a) cursed

b) accused

c) blamed

1167. It was snowing very … so I took my car.

a) wet

b) badly

c) hard

1168. He was … twenty euros for parking the car illegally.

a) fined

b) punished

c) charged

1169. Do you know what time the train … to Madrid?

a) gets

b) comes

c) reaches

1170. She never turned … at the cinema.

a) out

b) up

c) in

1171. The man … to give the police any more information.

a) objected

b) refused

c) disliked

1172. Can you give me … information about it?

a) any

b) all

c) one

1173. The boy was the only person to … the crash.

a) alive

b) survive

c) cure

1174. I have always been fond … games.

a) with

b) about

c) of

1175. I heard her … to John about holiday plans.

a) talk

b) talked

c) to talk

1176. These sweaters are … by this local firm.

a) well made

b) well-knit

c) well-founded

1177. Many undergraduates think it's east to … a job once they leave university.

a) collect

b) obtain

c) apply

1178. Brian is sucking up to the manager. I guess he's … for promotion.

a) acting

b) adhering

c) angling

1179. Her poetry is rather vague and … .

a) lucid

b) opaque

c) straightforward

1180. As rich as … . This phrase means extremely rich.

a) honey

b) Croesus

c) nails

1181. I ran … the thief, but I didn't catch him.

a) over

b) after

c) near

1182. Could you … me to take back those books?

a) remind

b) remember

c) memorize

1183. The new play is worth … .

a) to see

b) to seeing

c) seeing

1184. I'm not surprised you failed. You … have worked harder.

a) must

b) would

c) should

1185. … no need to buy a car.

a) You're

b) It has

c) There's

1186. She retired early … ill-health.

a) ahead of

b) in front of

c) on account of

1187. … did I have a sore throat, I also felt quite sick.

a) Not only

b) Also

c) In addition

1188. Do you think you could … me $25?

a) let

b) lend

c) borrow

1189. He is … a lot of money in his new job.

a) having

b) earning

c) gaining

1190. She was … of stealing one of the office laptops.

a) judged

b) charged

c) accused

1191. He tried harder than …, but he failed again.

a) ever

b) never

c) better

1192. Traffic is being … because of the parade.

a) altered

b) converted

c) diverted

1193. Don't blame him … this mess.

a) to

b) for

c) at

1194. Mary often suffers … colds.

a) at

b) on

c) from

1195. My competitor ran so fast I couldn't catch up … him.

a) to

b) from

c) with

1196. She has never done any work. She lives … her mother.

a) on

b) from

c) at

1197. His reports … in its remarks on the issue.

a) pulls no punches

b) pulls no needles

c) puts no punches

1198. My car … in the street.

a) has parked

b) is parked

c) had parked

1199. It's probably that the final price will … .

a) relax

b) evolved

c) escalate

1200. When the old lady tried to walk she had a sharp … in her leg.

a) hurt

b) pain

c) cut

1201. She stood on one leg, … against the wall.

a) leaning

b) stopping

c) staying

1202. … of all of us who are here tonight, thank you.
a) In person
b) On account
c) On behalf

1203. It was a mere …; I didn't mean to hurt them!
a) chance
b) accident
c) error

1204. When I was there my money … .
a) were stolen
b) was stealing
c) was stolen

1205. … to an accident, traffic is moving extremely slowly.
a) Because
b) Since
c) Owing

1206. I need to have a short rest as I … a headache.
a) take
b) have
c) feel

1207. Ducks fly in a definite … .
a) formation
b) formula
c) figure

1208. The police are looking … the matter.
a) up to
b) in on
c) into

1209. She must be … for 80.
a) going by
b) going off
c) getting on

1210. The sky is … so we can go fishing.
a) clean
b) clear
c) open

1211. It tasted so … of lemon. I didn't like it.

a) hardly

b) strongly
c) fully

1212. We are not in the least … about his opinion.
a) concerned
b) interested
c) aware

1213. Whenever you go to the sales, you … your money.
a) miss
b) leave
c) waste

1214. Paris lies … the Seine river.
a) on
b) over
c) at

1215. At the end of the day I watch a little TV … going to bed.
a) then
b) upon
c) before

1216. She decided to … early.
a) retire
b) resign
c) retreat

1217. It's obvious to us that the manager is not responsible … this mistake.
a) for
b) of
c) about

1218. The officer's orders were perfectly … .
a) exercised
b) executed
c) applied

1219. I'm going to get a top job soon. I'm a real high … .
a) cats
b) flier
c) market

1220. The girl takes … her mother.

a) over
b) for
c) after
1221. The … thing about travelling by train is that you can sleep.
a) enjoyed
b) enjoyable
c) enjoyment
1222. I let it ring several times before I … the receiver.
a) raised up
b) picked up
c) took out
1223. I have arranged special insurance to cover medical … .
a) expenses
b) prices
c) money
1224. You will be given an intelligence … during today's interview.
a) fitting
b) proof
c) test
1225. If you hear the baby … please call me.
a) say
b) cry
c) shout
1226. In the last months, a record number of cars … .
a) have been sold
b) have sold
c) had been sold
1227. Tim thought … getting a new job for a long time.
a) at
b) on
c) about
1228. I'm a millionaire … I expect everyone in this club to be a millionaire too.
a) then

b) but

c) and
1229. I'm disgusted … your behaviour!
a) to
b) for
c) at
1230. You forgot to thank her … the present.
a) for
b) on
c) at
1231. She's not fond … dancing.
a) at
b) of
c) on
1232. I was afraid of mentioning it … him.
a) on
b) for
c) to
1233. They have a … future ahead with little comfort and food.
a) grim
b) cruel
c) fierce
1234. Sarah … me all about her new job next Friday.
a) will tell
b) told
c) tells
1235. Mike … for Germany last weekend.
a) has left
b) had left
c) left
1236. I would have bought that PC, if I … money.
a) had have
b) had had
c) have had

1237. As soon as you … to the place, call me.
a) will get
b) has got
c) get
1238. If I had more time, I … some of those studies.
studies.

a) will read
b) would read
c) had read
1239. I'd be … to go to China one day.
a) interested
b) fond
c) helpful
1240. The product is a success. We're doing a
roaring … in it.
a) ship
b) deal
c) trade
1241. I shouldn't imagine there is … in this
organization who can answer
that question.
a) anyone
b) no one
c) somebody
1242. Here they learn how to get … with other
people.
a) away
b) along
c) across
1243. Hello. Please put me … to the marketing
manager.
a) up
b) over
c) through
1244. … pleasant it is to sit here in the garden!
a) So
b) How
c) What
1245. I'm going to … my suit cleaned.
a) make

b) send
c) have
1246. I'm afraid his writing is becoming more
and more … .
a) illegible
b) illiterate
c) eligible

1247. I had to … some trees so that I could
extend my herbs plantation.
a) cut
b) cut down
c) cut off
1248. I … rather not go there.
a) would
b) will
c) should
1249. Thank goodness you have come …!
a) finally
b) at the end
c) at last
1250. It was an unique car which must have
belonged to a … person.
a) plentiful
b) expensive
c) wealthy
1251. I'll give him your message the … I see
him.
a) minute
b) soon
c) time
1252. I had a … problem with my laptop.
a) like
b) same
c) similar
1253. She is quite stubborn, so it will be
difficult to … her to go.
a) suggest
b) persuade
c) make

1254. In the city park the officer came face …
face with the thief.
a) to
b) for
c) by
1255. I can't afford a laptop so we'll just have to
do … one.
a) down
b) up with
c) without

1256. I am intent … passing the exam.
a) with
b) to
c) on
1257. … the evening we will meet again.
a) In
b) About
c) On
1258. When I was washing the car, the telephone … .
a) would wing
b) rings
c) rang
1259. The bank is obliged to refuse your application for an extended … .
a) estimate
b) overdraft
c) balance
1260. The delay was brought … by bad weather.
a) up
b) down
c) about
1261. Jane … the office when I arrived.
a) was leaving
b) has left
c) leaves
1262. I will do the work and then send you the … for it.
a) sum

b) note
c) bill
1263. She seems to be … of leaving the house on time. She is always late.
a) unable
b) incapable
c) unaware
1264. She would not … her boyfriend's advice.
a) follow
b) agree
c) want
1265. She has never been too friendly to her colleagues and keeps them at a

… .
a) space
b) reserve
c) distance
1266. I … rather go to Spain than Russia for my holiday.
a) would
b) had
c) did
1267. Our organization is a small one with only a few … .
a) employees
b) employs
c) employers
1268. Catching this flight will give us the … to do some shopping.
a) luck
b) occasion
c) opportunity
1269. I've … had time to read the report. I can't give an opinion on it.
a) nearly
b) hardly
c) hard
1270. You … have rushed to the airport. The plane was delayed.
a) needn't
b) mustn't
c) couldn't

1271. They have helped the tourist business … .
a) no end
b) on end
c) at an end
1272. She looked embarrassed … than pleased.
a) apart
b) instead
c) rather
1273. I have been waiting for this day for years, and at … it has come.
a) the end
b) last
c) the finish

1274. This year the company made a … but next year I hope to make a

small profit.

a) loss

b) lose

c) loose

1275. The old man was cruel … his dog.

a) for

b) with

c) to

1276. I expect a great deal … you, Daniel.

a) on

b) from

c) at

1277. Mary is very efficient … her work.

a) on

b) with

c) at

1278. If he … me to do it, I would do so.

a) asks

b) asked

c) has asked

1279. I don't believe that this preposterous plan is … of our consideration.

a) worthy

b) worth

c) worthless

1280. They say Mary is an excellent manager. She runs a tight … .

a) deal

b) ship

c) bargain

1281. The gun fell into the river and was … along by the fast current.

a) caught

b) swept

c) thrown

1282. There is a lot of … when fruit and vegetables are not sold because

they are scraped.

a) rot

b) ruin

c) waste

1283. Why don't you look it … the dictionary?

a) up

b) at

c) in

1284. Do I have to make that course? No, you … .

a) haven't

b) mustn't

c) needn't

1285. I had no way of making a fire so I had to eat the meat … .

a) crude

b) rude

c) raw

1286. My plane takes … at 4 p.m.

a) out

b) off

c) up

1287. The child was told to … for being rude.

a) apologize

b) excuse

c) forgive

1288. I'll have to … to you. I don't want him to hear.

a) whisper

b) shout

c) say

1289. I'll call … you at 7 o'clock.

a) up

b) for

c) in

1290. Try to write the report the way Jane … .

a) puts

b) makes

c) does

1291. The concert was so … that I almost fell asleep.

a) boring

b) bored

c) tired

1292. When he entered the room, Mike looked rather pale and in … of a
shave.
a) lack
b) need
c) necessity
1293. The traffic lights … to green.
a) removed
b) shone
c) turned
1294. There were people who escaped … prison camps.
a) from
b) off
c) in
1295. How long have you been working … this project?
a) to
b) in
c) at
1296. I hope she won't … his offer.
a) have Steve up on

b) take Steve up on
c) get Steve up on
1297. After I had discussed my plans with him, I … to work on my project.
a) have started
b) started
c) would start

Set 12

1298. Absenteeism per employee in our company … out at 7 days per year.
a) averages
b) acts
c) arrives
1299. The storm played … with these houses.
a) down
b) havoc
c) along

1300. If you have a … of cards, I can show you a trick.
a) packet
b) set
c) pack
1301. This is the … of the laptop which was stolen.
a) detail
b) example
c) description
1302. It is … unlikely that the new manager will agree to that.
a) highly
b) mainly
c) greatly
1303. I've grown … to the noise of the trains.
a) familiar
b) accustomed
c) aware
1304. He … me of the first time we met.
a) reminded
b) recalled
c) remained

1305. The noise got … as the bike disappeared into the fog.
a) smaller
b) slighter
c) fainter
1306. … of all colleagues, I would like to wish you a happy retirement.
a) In place
b) On account
c) On behalf
1307. While studying, she depended … her family for money.
a) on
b) of
c) from
1308. Never before … seen such an enormous cake.
a) I had
b) had I

c) I have

1309. I wish she … her phone number before she left.

a) gave

b) would give

c) had given

1310. She always refuses … advice of any kind.

a) accepting

b) to reject

c) to accept

1311. I apologize … keeping you waiting so long.

a) for

b) from

c) with

1312. I appealed … her for help.

a) for

b) by

c) to

1313. The man is responding to treatment and will soon be cured … his illness.

a) from

b) of

c) with

1314. In the sky a … of birds was flying southward.

a) pack

b) swarm

c) flock

1315. A general manager … over all employees.

a) has ultimate authority

b) is an ultimate authority

c) is having ultimate authority

1316. It was … a hot tea that I burnt my mouth.

a) such

b) so

c) so and so

1317. I … to read this book before I found an interesting review about it.

a) had told

b) was told

c) had been told

1318. As I was … through the newspaper this morning I saw a picture of her.

a) staring

b) gazing

c) glancing

1319. Many of his remarks were derogatory and … lawsuits against him.

a) came upon

b) resulted in

c) assuaged

1320. There is no … that the new policy has been in any way disastrous.

a) indiscretion

b) indication

c) inducement

1321. When she retired from the job, the manager … Jane with a symbolic gift.

a) offered

b) presented

c) pleased

1322. The boat was … without trace during the storm.

a) crashed

b) vanished

c) lost

1323. … she comes, don't forget to call me.

a) If

b) In case

c) That

1324. He's the …-looking man I have ever met, said Mary about me.

a) most

b) best

c) well

1325. You can always count … me.

a) in

b) by

c) on

1326. My favourite … is roast chicken.

a) eat
b) dish
c) menu
1327. At seven o'clock, the old man still had some … to do in the garden.
a) job
b) task
c) work
1328. I … dark chocolate to white chocolate.
a) prefer
b) want
c) like
1329. You can't have this toy back … you promise to be a good boy.
a) when
b) until
c) while

1330. There was so … noise that I could hardly understand anything.
a) many
b) much
c) plentiful
1331. If you want to have a cat you must be ready to look … it for some time.
a) after
b) at
c) for
1332. She wishes she could … smoking.
a) give away
b) give from
c) give up
1333. The United States … from voting.
a) abstained
b) refused
c) rejected
1334. Don't worry. She always comes … time.
a) in
b) on
c) at
1335. My best friend confessed to me that he had been converted …another religion.
a) on
b) for
c) to
1336. You must have avoided risking …!
a) the life of your soldiers
b) the lives of your soldiers
c) your soldiers' life
1337. Before I decided to buy a plane ticket I … to wife.
a) had talked
b) talked
c) has talked

1338. I'm fed up to the back … with this pandemic.
a) ceiling
b) teeth
c) handle
1339. Given her … the manager's decision, she has no choice but to resign.
a) antipathy towards
b) pretense of
c) support for
1340. I like you because you aren't afraid to tackle … subjects.
a) concurrent
b) consecutive
c) controversial
1341. A crazy driver cut … so suddenly that I had to brake hard.
a) in
b) out
c) by
1342. If she … a little harder, her results would be better now.
a) works
b) worked
c) has worked
1343. The lights … out and we were left in darkness.
a) turned
b) put

c) went

1344. I had no … that the divorce rate was so high.

a) doubt

b) knowledge

c) idea

1345. I don't think he will … the shock of his sister's death.

a) get over

b) get through

c) get by

1346. … he is over seventy, Mr. Smith still goes jogging every day.

a) Despite

b) Unless

c) Although

1347. In today's newspaper it … that a coronavirus cure has been discovered.

a) notices

b) says

c) writes

1348. There is a large park … to the station. You will find an empty space.

a) across

b) close

c) right

1349. Seeing the room, I was … and complained to the manager about it.

a) disgusted

b) ashamed

c) disgusting

1350. … from anything else, he is always late.

a) As well

b) Except

c) Apart

1351. You should keep your dog on a … in this park.

a) lead

b) line

c) link

1352. Margaret has said that she will … the ceremony.

a) engage

b) impart

c) attend

1353. I'm not sure that this is … a good idea after all.

a) as

b) such

c) so

1354. They were unprepared … the news.

a) to

b) at

c) for

1355. The employees have embarked … a new scheme.

a) on

b) with

c) at

1356. What does this drink consist …?

a) with

b) from

c) of

1357. … I had to stand.

a) There's being no seats left

b) There being no seats left

c) There are no seats left

1358. I refused to give up work, … I'd won a big prize.

a) despite

b) however

c) even though

1359. We believe that the latest project will … expectations.

a) undermine

b) succeed

c) surpass

1360. It's distressing to see a kid … in the street.

a) begging

b) pleading

c) imploring

1361. The manager explained that he hoped to … new procedures to save time and money.
a) manufacture
b) control
c) establish

1362. Medicines should be kept out of the … of children.
a) hold
b) reach
c) grasp

1363. The manager … the employees to return to work.
a) ordered

b) insisted
c) suggested

1364. On holiday, I … always on the beach.
a) be
b) were
c) am

1365. Travelling to Moscow … air is quicker than driving.
a) by
b) on
c) over

1366. I'm not going to help you with your project and neither … Steve.
a) isn't
b) is
c) is going to

1367. … is a very good exercise, said the doctor.
a) To swim
b) A swim
c) Swimming

1368. The detective … to open a window at the back of the house.
a) managed
b) forced
c) succeeded

1369. I … going to the concert. It was marvelous.

a) hated
b) wanted
c) enjoyed

1370. She noticed the old lady … to get out of bed.
a) has tried
b) trying
c) tried

1371. Although the town had changed, much of it was still … to me.
a) common
b) relative
c) familiar

1372. If you want to change the item, make sure that you keep the … .
a) ticket
b) bill
c) notice

1373. When are they going to sell that car? Didn't you know? They decided … .
a) not to
b) not to be
c) not

1374. After the officers had questioned him for days, he broke … and confessed.
a) up
b) down
c) out

1375. While studying she was financially dependent … her husband.
a) to
b) of
c) on

1376. Luckily, I remembered … up with diesel.
a) to fill
b) filling
c) filled

1377. I've looked … the phone everywhere, but I can't find it.
a) at

b) on

c) for

1378. This country is well-known for its impressive mountainous … .

a) views

b) scenery

c) scene

1379. If they … to that event, they would attend it.

a) were invited

b) are invited

c) will be invited

1380. I will lend you this book collection next month if I … it.

a) am reading

b) were read

c) finish reading

1381. Our house is … at the corner of a busy street.

a) stood

b) situated

c) stood

1382. If I were you I … go to the doctor.

a) could

b) will

c) would

1383. The new chimney was … than all the trees around it.

a) longer

b) taller

c) deeper

1384. The police officer … me $10 for parking there.

a) fined

b) asked

c) demanded

1385. His mother was very … because he was out so late that night.

a) sorry

b) worried

c) overcome

1386. Take a toothbrush just in … .

a) time

b) order

c) case

1387. The answer … higher employment is a greater production.

a) for

b) with

c) to

1388. We meet for dinner … every Friday.

a) hourly

b) up to date

c) at the same time

1389. On the … to the woods there is a beautiful restaurant.

a) way

b) direction

c) street

1390. We don't have any … sizes in stock.

a) higher

b) larger

c) greater

1391. The patient … to listen to doctor's advice.

a) lacked

b) hindered

c) refused

1392. Children with … diseases should not be allowed to go to school.

a) infectious

b) contact

c) influential

1393. … twenty minutes of the game one player had been sent off.

a) Before

b) Inside

c) Within

1394. It happened … I was asleep.

a) while

b) during

c) for

Set 13

1395. It's obvious … everyone that she's not responsible for this situation.
a) at
b) from
c) to

1396. His … for the services was a seat in the Cabinet.
a) reward
b) repayment
c) recompense

1397. The documents need … .
a) sorting out
b) sorting off
c) sorting out of

1398. I hope the project … by next month.
a) has been finished
b) had been finished
c) will have been finished

1399. I don't know the answer but I will … around.
a) attend
b) ask
c) accord

1400. I thought the way my cousin behaved was … outrageous.
a) very
b) extremely
c) quite

1401. The only way to clean this is to … it in soap and warm water.
a) polish
b) wash
c) wipe

1402. It's … to rain again today.
a) likely
b) possibly
c) probably

1403. The little girl hasn't … her shyness yet.
a) got under
b) get through

c) get over

1404. The store gave me a 10 per cent … for paying cash.
a) sale
b) discount
c) bargain

1405. My leg was very … after the wasp stung me.
a) swollen
b) wide
c) thick

1406. … I have a beer, please?
a) Must
b) Shall
c) Could

1407. They met yesterday to discuss the … at the factory.
a) closing
b) block
c) strike

1408. I was unable to warn you because my telephone was … .
a) off duty
b) out of order
c) out of work

1409. Don't … her to arrive early.
a) expect
b) judge
c) think

1410. Sometimes I can't … the professor.
a) keep at
b) keep up to
c) keep up with

1411. The car broke … on my way there so I wasn't able to be on time.
a) up
b) down
c) in

1412. He signed the agreement … the General Manager.
a) on behalf of
b) because of

c) on account of

1413. Who is going to pay … this mess?

a) on

b) in

c) for

1414. He is jealous … his older brother.

a) to

b) at

c) of

1415. She might be good … her job, but I can't rely on her.

a) at

b) in

c) on

1416. I felt considerably … after a meal and a rest.

a) renewed

b) refreshed

c) remade

1417. My eldest sister intends to take … skiing next winter.

a) up

b) to

c) away

1418. The bank … planned to escape using a plane.

a) thieves

b) robbers

c) bandits

1419. Which soldier is … this morning?

a) on call

b) on the call

c) at call

1420. Your laziness and … could result in your dismissal.

a) ambition

b) zeal

c) procrastination

1421. Tom is stubborn, so it will be difficult to … him to go.

a) make

b) suggest

c) persuade

1422. When the time came to … the bill she left.

a) pay

b) pay out

c) pay up

1423. The film … several scenes that might upset some people.

a) admits

b) contains

c) involves

1424. My house is going to be knocked … when the new highway is built.

a) out

b) down

c) away

1425. I returned the laptop to he shop because it was … .

a) mistaken

b) wrong

c) faulty

1426. Can you come here? I … speak to you about something.

a) must

b) can

c) should

1427. I've never had to … such things before.

a) get out of

b) put up with

c) go off with

1428. I don't think I have … eaten something like this before.

a) always

b) rarely

c) ever

1429. We all felt sorry … her.

a) with

b) for

c) about

1430. Which … choose between these two?

a) do your rather

b) would you rather

c) did you rather

1431. Everything was …, just like any other
day.
a) normal
b) average
c) common
1432. The mechanic … me $10 for mending my
bicycle.
a) asked
b) demanded
c) charged
1433. … I tell you yesterday not to go there?
a) Hasn't
b) Didn't
c) Haven't
1434. Inflation and its upward … is worrying.
a) bend
b) stream
c) trend
1435. I apologized for causing so much … .
a) problem
b) trouble
c) damage
1436. I am … to come to the meeting.
a) capable
b) excused
c) unable
1437. I suppose I can count … you for help?
a) on
b) in
c) from
1438. We began by experimenting … rats.
a) of
b) in
c) on
1439. I bought the land with a … to building a
new office.
a) purpose

b) goal
c) view
1440. In all … there will never be a third World
War.

a) odds
b) probability
c) certainty
1441. The defendant's wife was present at the
… .
a) court
b) hearing
c) law
1442. I don't … with your decision. It's fine.
a) disagree
b) displease
c) dislike
1443. … I lock the door?
a) Will
b) Need
c) Shall
1444. My car was badly … in the accident.
a) hurt
b) damaged
c) broken
1445. Come … instead of standing on the
doorstep.
a) in
b) to
c) by
1446. Everyone in the city … about the plans
for the new road.
a) was concerned
b) took care
c) had concerned
1447. I … my friends to go camping with me.
a) attracted
b) suggested
c) persuaded

1448. What needs …?
a) to do
b) to be done
c) to be doing
1449. I ... my family very much when I'm away
from home.
a) miss
b) lack

c) long

1450. The … age of the population is rising.

a) medium

b) general

c) average

1451. You can't get these pills unless you go to the doctor and get a … .

a) receipt

b) prescription

c) recipe

1452. Driving a bike with faulty brakes is … quite a risk.

a) taking

b) putting

c) setting

1453. The assistant apologized and said that she didn't have any of them …
yet.

a) in stock

b) in store

c) out of stock

1454. You … have passed that exam. I believe you didn't work hard
enough.

a) must

b) should

c) can

1455. Jennifer hadn't seen her brother for twenty years and … she
recognized him.

a) so

b) despite

c) yet

1456. You … be exhausted after that mission.

a) must

b) can

c) need

1457. These pills are round, so they're easier to
… .

a) eat

b) chew

c) swallow

1458. I … myself and left the party. It was late.

a) refused

b) excused

c) thanked

1459. Do you … to go to the meeting?

a) pretend

b) attempt

c) intend

1460. I … the plumber to install an extra radiator.

a) arranged

b) got

c) intend

1461. I'm free this evening. … we go out to dinner?

a) Will

b) Shall

c) Won't

1462. The officer threw the drowning woman a lifebelt in the … of time.

a) nick

b) end

c) quick

1463. Children have to stay … school until 1 p.m.

a) with

b) on

c) at

1464. The management received a lot of … about the service.

a) information

b) advice

c) complaints

1465. It has been raining for five days … now.

a) at an end

b) on end

c) in the end

1466. The opening … of the play took place in camp.

a) stage

b) sight

c) scene

1467. I don't know what to do this Saturday.
Perhaps I … at home and so
some work.
a) stay
b) will stay
c) am staying
1468. When you … the Smiths, give them my
best wishes.
a) will visit
b) would visit
c) visit
1469. The sign asks people … smoke.
a) not to
b) to not
c) don't
1470. He never became the … of the local chess
club, despite his
intelligence.
a) member
b) champion
c) winner
1471. … for Adam, we enjoyed the play very
much.
a) Except
b) Apart
c) Aside
1472. Mary is unemployed. She'd feel much
happier if she were in … .
a) touch

b) job
c) work
1473. Five meters of this material … at $35.
a) add up
b) fetch down
c) work out
1474. It was difficult to … a date which was
convenient for us.
a) elect
b) arrange
c) organize
1475. There was nothing I could do … leave the
car there.

a) unless
b) but
c) instead of
1476. Did anything emerge … your meeting?
a) from
b) on
c) of
1477. You can't rely … Steve. He's away on
holiday all the time.
a) at
b) on
c) with
1478. The concert began … a new instrumental
song.
a) on
b) in
c) with
1479. When I realized it was three o'clock, I
stopped … a rest.
a) having
b) have
c) had
1480. Are you … to leave?
a) thinking
b) planned
c) about

1481. The soldier … a dangerous mission.
a) undertook
b) agreed
c) entered
1482. What a lovely suit … on!
a) have you
b) you've got
c) have you got
1483. They have just released a new graphic
card, … you must buy.
a) that
b) what
c) which
1484. Because nobody admitted breaking the
windows, the … class was
punished.

a) all
b) whole
c) each
1485. It was a good attempt, but it didn't really come … .
a) off
b) on
c) away
1486. Your test result is poor, … you have failed.
a) because
b) therefore
c) however
1487. Would you … talking a little bit more quietly?
a) care
b) rather
c) mind
1488. The bank seems to have credited my account with $500 in … .
a) error
b) fortune
c) accident
1489. I'm sorry but I don't … you at all.
a) agree to

b) disagree to
c) agree with
1490. This wine is cheap but it is very … .
a) drinking
b) drinkable
c) drank
1491. Do you … bringing your laptop? Mine is broken.
a) mind
b) complain
c) oppose
1492. She has a … temper and often says things, which she later regrets.
a) warm
b) angry
c) quick
1493. The child says he's sorry … what he did.

a) of
b) for
c) from
1494. I'm satisfied … your project.
a) with
b) to
c) at
1495. She cannot be held responsible … other people's mistakes.
a) by
b) to
c) for
1496. I will ask him to return my book when I … him.
a) see
b) saw
c) will see
1497. My speech may have … you.
a) mistaken
b) misled
c) miscalculated

1498. What she told me was a … of lies.
a) load
b) pack
c) flock
1499. The death penalty was … two years ago in this country.
a) absolved
b) aborted
c) abolished
1500. Stop … yourself. Your work is highly valued.
a) belittling
b) interpreting
c) distinguishing
1501. Food prices have been … steadily for the last two years.
a) lifting
b) rising
c) raising
1502. I'll have to study hard, … I can pass the exam.

a) in order
b) such
c) so that
1503. You … to drink if you don't feel like it.
a) don't have
b) haven't
c) mustn't
1504. We'll play football and … we'll have a drink.
a) then
b) so
c) straight away
1505. She has to go to Berlin for the next … of her training.
a) step
b) stage
c) stand
1506. After the meeting had finished, we went … the project once again.
a) over

b) up
c) on
1507. I locked the bird in a cage to … it from getting away.
a) avoid
b) hinder
c) prevent
1508. You're … your time trying to persuade her.
a) losing
b) wasting
c) missing
1509. Out last cook was better than the … one.
a) former
b) current
c) latter
1510. I am grateful to you for being so patient … me.
a) with
b) at
c) for

1511. Do you mean to say you exchanged that performant laptop … this?
a) for
b) on
c) to
1512. The rain floods were … the poor harvest.
a) accused of
b) blamed for
c) condemned for
1513. I have so many things to get done today. …, I have to finish this boring project.
a) At top
b) At the top of
c) On top of it
1514. I don't see any … in arriving that early.
a) cause
b) aim
c) point

1515. His application was turned … by the consulate.
a) down
b) out
c) over
1516. This is a controlled environment which … concerns about the weather.
a) foster
b) necessitate
c) eliminate
1517. It is … impossible to tell the twins apart at this age.
a) virtually
b) closely
c) extremely
1518. Thomas claimed that he was the … heir to the throne.
a) due
b) rightful
c) correct
1519. This aspect in no way … from the beauty of the place.

a) protracts
b) attracts
c) detracts
1520. … no need to do it again.
a) There's
b) You're
c) It has
1521. Some colleagues only read the … lines in a newspaper.
a) top
b) head
c) main
1522. You should always check the sell … date of the products you buy.
a) by
b) in
c) off
1523. When the project was completed, the workers were paid … .
a) out

b) over
c) off
1524. The manager was good enough to … our mistakes.
a) overlook
b) overtake
c) overdo
1525. It is … when you misunderstand something.
a) singular
b) attitude
c) embarrassing
1526. Magazines are … to their door every day.
a) taken
b) delivered
c) handed

Set 14

1527. She expressed her … for all the help.
a) thanking
b) gratitude

c) gratefulness
1528. In … nothing happened at the meeting.
a) short
b) quick
c) briefly
1529. The assembly gave the speaker a standing … .
a) applause
b) support
c) ovation
1530. Local politicians pretend to ignore opinion … .
a) votes
b) polls
c) numbers
1531. Start reading the story from page 20 and then go on until you … the end of the book.
a) arrive
b) touch
c) reach

1532. Make … that you check your ideas carefully.
a) definite
b) sure
c) clear
1533. The purpose of these exercises is to … your knowledge and enhance it.
a) prone
b) interpret
c) test
1534. A useful way to … your vocabulary is to read more.
a) increase
b) amass
c) gather
1535. You can also read novels so that you can see examples of … language.
a) automatic
b) axiomatic

c) idiomatic
1536. An important activity is to … your spoken language.
a) train
b) practise
c) exercise
1537. It's very good if you can … the cost of travelling to that country.
a) afford
b) spend
c) expend
1538. Try to … a native speaker to talk to you. I challenge you!
a) influence
b) impress
c) persuade
1539. Play the recording and … everything she said.
a) hold
b) repeat
c) take

1540. It won't be long before you find yourself speaking the language … .
a) fluently
b) frequently
c) flowingly
1541. You have to … a form and send it to my secretary.
a) fill out
b) fill up
c) fill into
1542. We'll have to wait a little longer because I'm sure he will … soon.
a) turn in
b) turn down
c) turn up
1543. Last week I … that perfume you wanted in a boutique.
a) came up
b) came across
c) came into

1544. I have to … a new idea that will enable me to make more money.
a) think up
b) think about
c) think over
1545. I need to find a chemical product that will … the weeds in my garden.
a) keep off
b) keep down
c) keep out
1546. In spring, people feel inclined to … their houses.
a) do over
b) do in
c) do up
1547. It will be necessary to … making a better plan.
a) see about
b) see over
c) see into
1548. It's easy to see from the way the forest is looking that winter has … .
a) set out

b) set in
c) set off
1549. I will always … you darling.
a) stand to
b) stand from
c) stand by
1550. By the way she talks and behaves it's clear that she … her mother.
a) takes after
b) takes to
c) takes back
1551. There's no need to worry. We have … of time.
a) parcels
b) bags
c) sacks
1552. The movie doesn't start at least an hour so I have time to … .
a) kill

b) murder

c) remove

1553. The station isn't far away. We have time to … .

a) save

b) store

c) spare

1554. With time on his … he is likely to get into trouble.

a) feet

b) hands

c) fingers

1555. I told her time and … not to do it.

a) often

b) already

c) again

1556. I like to get to an appointment in … time.

a) best

b) good

c) fine

1557. It's … time she learnt to cook.

a) of

b) in

c) about

1558. I'm not living here for good; just for the time … .

a) being

b) seeing

c) trying

1559. Time … ; it's difficult to believe that I've been here all day.

a) flows

b) flees

c) files

1560. Time will … whether I have made the right decision.

a) say

b) find

c) tell

1561. Our business has lost a lot of orders and is going through a … time.

a) thin

b) slender

c) poor

1562. The trains always arrive … time in this country.

a) for

b) at

c) on

1563. I think they are merely playing … time.

a) at

b) for

c) in

1564. This company is well … the times.

a) behind

b) across

c) under

1565. Her invention proved she was … of her time.

a) before

b) forward

c) ahead

1566. You can tell Tom has hit the … time because of the car he drives.

a) high

b) large

c) big

1567. It's … time you went to the post office.

a) quick

b) high

c) proper

1568. The artists are meant to … time with the conductor.

a) take

b) keep

c) show

1569. If you want to grow your business you must … with the times.

a) move

b) hold

c) follow

1570. The parcel arrived two weeks later and not … time.

a) after

b) for

c) before

1571. Before applying for a job you should be sure that you have the right

paper … .

a) qualities

b) qualifiers

c) qualifications

1572. You should work out the … you have in mind for the ideal employee.

a) picture

b) profile

c) sketch

1573. As soon as the … arrive for the interview it will be your job to show

them around.

a) candidates

b) chosen

c) appliers

1574. The company is doing an advertising campaign with a view to …

new staff.

a) taking

b) recruiting

c) reaching

1575. After you've read the details of the job …

your application.

a) pursue

b) submit

c) undertake

1576. Do you expect her to … with a cost cutting scheme?

a) come over

b) come by

c) come up

1577. You've chosen a good industry to seek employment in because I've

heard that jobs are … there.

a) many

b) frequent

c) plenty

1578. It can be a time … process but it's worth in the end.

a) lasting

b) consuming

c) taking

1579. It's relevant to discuss a candidate's … at previous jobs.

a) deeds

b) doings

c) accomplishments

1580. I can offer you a salary that will be … with the responsibilities.

a) equal

b) level

c) commensurate

1581. He was able to … the cause of her headaches.

a) decide

b) diagnose

c) define

1582. It was beyond my capability and I … the patient to a specialist.

a) referred

b) reduced

c) returned

1583. The doctor reassured Steve that his condition was not … .

a) clear

b) possible

c) serious

1584. The dentist took out of her bag an unusual … but promised her

patient that it wouldn't hurt.

a) utensil

b) instrument

c) control

1585. The prescribed medication has been … .

a) effective

b) effects

c) effecting

1586. If you cancel your … and don't notify the clinic you will be fined.

a) meeting

b) rendezvous

c) appointment

1587. A specialist had to … the extent of her mobility.

a) assess

b) assume

c) accept

1588. The treatment has proved successful but he has to arrange to visit the
doctor's … .

a) always

b) annually

c) usually

1589. It's much easier to … an illness than to cure it.

a) prevent   b) prepare   c) prefer

Set 14

1590. We had to write to the previous hospital so as to obtain his … .

a) writings

b) recordings

c) records

1591. Perhaps you could start by telling me why you've … .

a) obtained for this job

b) applied for this job

c) asked for this job

1592. Steve likes working in … .

a) the free air

b) the pure air

c) the open air

1593. Do you like the idea of an office with …?

a) air control

b) air condition

c) air conditioning

1594. I don't understand what you're … .

a) on about

b) in about

c) for about

1595. I thought this was … obvious.

a) pretty

b) mostly

c) clear

1596. To me, … obvious at all.

a) it can't be

b) it won't be

c) it isn't

1597. I think there must be a mistake. I … .

a) put it you're Mr. Smith

b) take it you're Mr. Smith

c) place it you're Mr. Smith

1598. I'm afraid it was a case of mistaken … .

a) personality

b) character

c) identity

1599. You're not after the job of police officer … .

a) I presume

b) I pretend

c) I preview

1600. I want to be a security guard … .

a) if you don't care

b) if you don't mind

c) if you don't see

1601. I am writing this e-mail to describe the … I've been having with this
product.

a) incidents

b) instances

c) problems

1602. I am talking about your latest laptop … in the January catalogue.

a) deferred

b) considered

c) described

1603. I want to take … over the name itself this time.

a) issue

b) trouble

c) pains

1604. "Shrewd" to my mind suggests …, which she doesn't possess.

a) wonderful
b) excellence
c) outstanding
1605. You should have thought it was an essential … of this system.
a) require
b) requirement
c) requires
1606. Unfortunately, this doesn't … to your product.
a) concern

b) attribute
c) apply
1607. One day, the lawnmower simply … over the grass but didn't cut it.
a) walked
b) tripped
c) strode
1608. …, I was wrong about it.
a) Confessing
b) Admitted
c) Admittedly
1609. I want you to pay me … my money!
a) return
b) again
c) back
1610. I someone to come and repair my laptop at your … .
a) expense
b) expenditure
c) expending
1611. I thought it was … time I called you.
a) at
b) about
c) in
1612. She has at long last … to marry Mike.
a) concerted
b) consented
c) convened
1613. We will be able to make an … man of him.
a) honest

b) honour
c) honestly
1614. I want to ask of you a very important … .
a) favouring
b) favourite
c) favour

1615. Putting it … I am delighted!
a) easily
b) simply
c) fairly
1616. I can … you that the duties are not in any way intricate.
a) assure
b) affirm
c) assert
1617. She is an … supporter.
a) arduous
b) ardent
c) articulate
1618. Why aren't you tying the …?
a) knot
b) rope
c) string
1619. I don't understand why I have to give up my … .
a) latitude
b) scope
c) liberty
1620. I wait for your … as soon as possible.
a) recur
b) respect
c) response
1621. I would like to … this application for the job.
a) deliver
b) submit
c) return
1622. As you can see from my … C.V. I have relevant experience.
a) attached
b) appeared
c) included

1623. This is a … job for someone who has been a manager.
a) stranger

b) unusually
c) peculiar
1624. You should explain the … reason for what you've done.
a) underlying
b) undercover
c) understanding
1625. It's the job of a sales consultant to … the clients into choosing from
the catalogue.
a) push
b) tempt
c) pervade
1626. I'm sure I could easily … all the requirements.
a) fulfill
b) commit
c) completed
1627. She cannot decide whether to have … fruit or tiramisu.
a) picked
b) wet
c) fresh
1628. Make sure you … the one we have most of.
a) decide
b) select
c) effect
1629. I am sure you can … your skills to the new employee.
a) transfer
b) translate
c) transverse
1630. I look forward to … from your company.
a) hear
b) hearing
c) heard
1631. We reached our … after a dramatic journey.

a) destination
b) end
c) aim

1632. She could say that she is having a wonderful time but that would be
… from the truth.
a) distant
b) long
c) far
1633. The airport had a problem because of the industrial … taken by the
baggage handlers.
a) acts
b) action
c) acting
1634. They decided they didn't want to … my case on to the helicopter.
a) lode
b) lead
c) load
1635. Sorry! I was held … for one hour.
a) up
b) by
c) on
1636. As you can … I was tired, hungry and miserable.
a) anticipate
b) think
c) imagine
1637. When I arrived at the motel I had to … my luggage.
a) sort out
b) sort in
c) sort of
1638. She wasn't there any mote. She had simply … .
a) distorted
b) dislodged
c) disappeared
1639. My first day was spent in local shops … for gifts.
a) finding

b) searching

c) purchasing

1640. The manager greeted us … from ear to ear.

a) streaming

b) screaming

c) beaming

1641. Do you have any idea what this …?

a) means

b) tells

c) says

1642. Apparently, it is an … . So the letters in the word are the first letters of a group of words.

a) addition

b) anomaly

c) acronym

1643. This acronym … the central building.

a) stands by

b) stands for

c) stands up

1644. The soldier jumped out of a plane 6.000 meters … the river.

a) up

b) higher

c) above

1645. She intended to … across the channel.

a) flee

b) flow

c) fly

1646. The pilot started early in the morning so that he was able to … commercial flights.

a) avoid

b) evict

c) eject

1647. During the race my supporters … that I reached 220 km/h.

a) attained

b) argued

c) claimed

1648. The fact remains that the terrorist … and managed to escape.

a) survived

b) lived

c) continued

1649. Wilma has created a new … by beating him.

a) recorder

b) record

c) recording

1650. The … is about 30 minutes.

a) duration

b) lasting

c) during

1651. Teaching someone to fly a plane is one of the … experiences you can have.

a) scariest

b) latest

c) cruelest

1652. I'm here to … you in driving a car.

a) learn

b) instruct

c) perform

1653. Be careful when you drive. You can end up in the … .

a) side

b) floor

c) ditch

1654. This is more … if the partner is a member of your family.

a) complicated

b) confused

c) confirmed

1655. The situation between you and your wife could end in … .

a) distance

b) diversion

c) divorce

1656. The secret of being a good teacher is never to lose your temper or your … .

a) brain

b) head

c) idea

1657. She might lose … of the car.

a) break

b) stop

c) control

1658. In my … none of what you've told happened.

a) case

b) example

c) instance

1659. I was proud of them because they all … the exam first time.

a) past

b) passing

c) passed

1660. The only … to me is where she is.

a) confusion

b) mystery

c) intrigue

1661. Those companies find themselves in a … situation.

a) precarious

b) pertinent

c) pretentious

1662. Whenever there is a meeting between them rumours … .

a) abut

b) about

c) abound

1663. They were judged for … the documents.

a) mistaking

b) misfiring

c) mishandling

1664. We want to … the concerns of our borrowers.

a) assert

b) assuage

c) assent

1665. Negotiations will eventually be … .

a) retaken

b) resumed

c) returned

1666. The government tries to convince everyone that it is … of all people.

a) supported

b) supportive

c) supporting

1667. Measures are due to come into … on Friday.

a) force

b) law

c) forcing

1668. Do you know when these laws will be …?

a) rating

b) ratified

c) rated

1669. This is very disappointing for the … car buyer.

a) would-see

b) would-go

c) would-be

1670. I have nothing of … to report.

a) notice

b) noted

c) note

1671. Suppose an … public figure attacked by press and public.

a) embattled

b) engrossed

c) empowered

1672. Any arguments he put up were regarded as a … .

a) cloud

b) fog

c) smokescreen

1673. Her protestations of innocence were wearing a bit … .

a) bare

b) thin

c) scarce

1674. Police forces were determined to … this kind of crime.

a) curb
b) manage
c) restrain
1675. This media trust was … to make publicity
about the candidate.
a) picked
b) proposed
c) prompted
1676. Mary spent a lot of time … the press on
this subject.
a) briefing
b) training
c) showing
1677. Views … from utter conviction that she
was guilty to wild support for
her innocence.
a) started
b) ranged
c) began
1678. Even his supporters were beginning to …
him.
a) despair
b) destroy
c) desert
1679. New evidence came to … proving she
was innocent.
a) light
b) see
c) show
1680. The incident … everything he did for the
rest of his life.
a) overlook
b) overcome
c) overshadowed
1681. Such a piece of information cannot be
released into the public … .
a) domain
b) domestic
c) dominion

1682. They run the risk of facing a … if they
break the official secrets act.
a) back store

b) back strike
c) backlash
1683. There is a … inquiry into specific
information.
a) high profile
b) high brow
c) high drama
1684. The more you try to conceal information
about an event, the more it
fuels … about it.
a) spectacle
b) speculation
c) speculative
1685. You will get … by authorities if you dare
reveal this report.
a) rave
b) savaged
c) wild
1686. The officer will … what can be disclosed.
a) sign
b) seal
c) signal
1687. Once the disclosure is … it's her job to
analyze the facts.
a) hightailed
b) heightened
c) highlighted
1688. The public can see through the … of a
weak argument.
a) clarity
b) clearness
c) transparency
1689. This is likely to … a threat to the safety of
the community.
a) start
b) pose
c) place
1690. This small country is a … for
troublemakers.
a) heaven

b) location
c) port

1691. Today the government is … plans for a new highway.
a) unveiling
b) opening
c) showing

1692. The plan is about trying to … stealing in the country.
a) kill
b) curb
c) confuse

1693. The new conference system will be … next academic year.
a) introduced
b) welcomed
c) enforced

1694. They should be taught to respect other people's property and … .
a) added
b) additions
c) belongings

1695. She will have to stand up in front of her colleagues and … to being a thief.
a) confess
b) conduce
c) conform

1696. The … said the Prime Minister was sick.
a) spoken person
b) spokesperson
c) speaking person

1697. Last month we had to give an important address to an international …
.
a) assembled
b) assembly
c) assembling

1698. … of the speech she told funny stories.
a) In case

b) Intend
c) Instead

1699. The audience didn't see the funny … of her stories.

a) edge
b) part
c) line

1700. The presenter cannot continue with the news because someone has … the next page.
a) misread
b) mistaken
c) misappropriated

Second set of items

1701. I take my hat … to the new manager for avoiding bankruptcy.
a) to
b) off
c) on

1702. She's not thinking straight. She's talking … her hat.
a) at
b) under
c) up

1703. This is a society wedding where men wear … hats and tails.
a) tall
b) full
c) long

1704. I'd like you to keep this information … your hat.
a) under
b) by
c) over

1705. She decided to throw her hat in the … and become a candidate.
a) circle
b) ring
c) middle

1706. If he wins I'll … my hat.
a) eat
b) consume
c) bite

1707. Steve changes his mind at the … of a hat.
a) jump
b) fall

c) drop

1708. That suit is … hat now.

a) gone

b) late

c) old

1709. I think it would be nice to … round the hat for him.

a) offer

b) hand

c) place

1710. There are so many responsibilities involved that she has to … several hats.

a) wear

b) take

c) put

1711. A salesperson should … potential customers of the usefulness of a product.

a) consider

b) confirm

c) convince

1712. You must believe in the product and be … enough to promote it.

a) included

b) indebted

c) inspired

1713. A … customer will return to the same firm and buy again.

a) satisfied

b) interested

c) encouraged

1714. That style of dress was once considered to be a … .

a) fuss

b) fad

c) fun

1715. We need to … a new product this year.

a) market

b) muster

c) maintain

1716. They watch the supermarkets … for the same clientele.

a) contrasting

b) confusing

c) competing

1717. Weekly meetings were not considered to be … enough.

a) produced

b) productive

c) products

1718. She is able to … facts and figures quickly.

a) consumer

b) consume

c) consuming

1719. On this website customers can … different prices for the same article.

a) continue

b) confer

c) compare

1720. If you want to keep … with the latest developments you have to read a lot.

a) current

b) currant

c) currents

1721. … every student passed the exam.

a) Near to

b) Next to

c) Nearly

1722. I can look back on my career with great … .

a) satisfied

b) satisfaction

c) satisfactory

1723. The captain, as well as the passengers, … frightened.

a) been

b) were

c) was

1724. Both of these girls … married.

a) are

b) have

c) has

1725. Each learner of a foreign language … a good dictionary.

a) need

b) is

c) needs

1726. Money, nor fame … brought happiness to everybody.

a) has

b) have

c) is

1727. I … at this university before I became an interpreter.

a) taught

b) had taught

c) were taught

1728. The salary of a truck driver is higher … .

a) than a teacher

b) than that of a teacher

c) to compare as a teacher

1729. Professionals expect you to call them when it is necessary … an appointment.

a) cancel

b) to cancel

c) canceled

1730. I have chosen this laptop because of its operation simplicity … its capacity to store information.

a) the same as

b) the same

c) as well as

1731. Many embarrassing situations occur … a misunderstanding.

a) for

b) because

c) because of

1732. This is an extremely cold planet and … .

a) so is Uranus

b) so does Neptune

c) so has Uranus

1733. … when gold was discovered in this area.

a) Because in 1850

b) It was in 1850

c) In 1850 it was

1734. This job has no … .

a) prospector

b) prospects

c) prospective

1735. Frost occurs in valleys … on adjacent hills.

a) more frequently than

b) as frequently than

c) frequently than

1736. The mountain can be … from more than 200 kilometers away.

a) see

b) saw

c) seen

1737. I'd like you … her family.

a) to meet

b) meet

c) meeting

1738. Mr. Smith along with his friends … arriving here tonight.

a) are

b) will

c) were

1739. You must listen very … in order to understand it.

a) care

b) careful

c) carefully

1740. Cold objects emit … hot ones.

a) fewer than infrared rays as

b) fewer infrared rays than

c) as fewer infrared rays

1741. Gunpowder … a mixture of potassium nitrate, charcoal and sulfur.

a) were

b) was

c) is

1742.This city has played a vital role in the industrial … .
a) developing
b) develop
c) development

1743. They … forced to make smaller cars to compete in the market.
a) will
b) are
c) should

1744. Jennifer has … the conditions for entry.
a) satisfied
b) satisfaction
c) satisfactory

1745. The person … was recommended by the manager to replace him is
Marry.
a) whose
b) who
c) which

1746. His fame rested on the breadth of his range, which was … any other
tenor.
a) greater than that of
b) as large as
c) more greater

1747. Words are constantly being invented … new objects and concepts.
a) describe
b) describing
c) to describe

1748. You can't … to learn a foreign language in a month.
a) expect
b) expectant
c) expected

1749. … rain or snow there are always fans at these football games.
a) In spite with   b) Despite of
          c) Despite

Set 15

1750. The prices are … high in urban areas that I can't afford a house.
a) as
b) so as
c) so

1751. To see the church and … pictures of it are two reasons for visiting
this city.
a) taken
b) to take
c) taking

1752. I can't see the … of sitting there all day.
a) attract
b) attractive
c) attractiveness

1753. This product is equal … to none.
a) as
b) to
c) with

1754. These bricks are much harder … that are dried in the sun.
a) those
b) ones
c) than those

1755. Since infection can cause … fever … pain, you must avoid it.
a) both/as well as
b) both/with
c) both/and

1756. Schizophrenia … by genetic predisposition, stress, drugs or infections.
a) may be triggered
b) may triggered
c) may trigger

1757. They asked us, Olivia and … about it.
a) I
b) me
c) my

1758. She was guilty … racial discrimination.

a) of

b) with

c) for

1759. It is important … it on because it is an expensive coat.

a) of trying

b) try

c) to try

1760. What happened in this city … a reaction from outskirts workers.

a) were

b) was

c) is

1761. The result of the drug experiment was … .

a) satisfactory

b) satisfied

c) satisfaction

1762. A number of … submitted their manuscripts under pseudonyms.

a) novel

b) novelists

c) novels

1763. I require that the secretary … responsible for writing all reports.

a) was

b) been

c) be

1764. Although a medical doctor may be able to diagnose a problem … he

may not be able to find a treatment.

a) perfect

b) perfectly

c) perfection

1765. This law is purely … .

a) prospective

b) prospect

c) prospector

1766. The number of days in a week … seven.

a) is

b) are

c) needs

1767. The nurses will not … you donate blood if you have just had a cold.

a) want

b) need

c) let

1768. This item has two parts: one made up of dust … made up of

electrically charged particles.

a) the other

b) one another

c) each other

1769. There were over fifty boats on the river, … were quire luxurious.

a) many of them

b) many of which

c) many that

1770. Columbus thought that he … the East Indies.

a) had reached

b) has reached

c) had been reached

1771. Most university leavers have the … to go to work.

a) keen

b) keenly

c) keenness

1772. It's good that … objections to the plan haven't happened.

a) expected

b) expectant

c) expect

1773. Many students are afraid … failing an exam.

a) about

b) of

c) to

1774. It is important that the office … your registration.

a) confirms

b) will confirm

c) need confirm

1775. Please state your name, age and … .

a) occupy
b) occupied
c) occupation
1776. Deserts are often formed … surrounding mountain ranges.
a) because
b) in spite of
c) so
1777. … that they settled in this area.
a) It was in 1000
b) That in 1000
c) In 1000 that it was
1778. Staying in a hotel costs … renting a room.
a) twice more than
b) twice as much as
c) as much twice as
1779. When friends insist on … expensive gifts it makes most people uncomfortable.
a) them to accept
b) they accept
c) their accepting
1780. Do any of these designs … you?
a) attractive
b) attract
c) attractively
1781. These flowers usually smell … .
a) sweet
b) sweetly
c) sweetness
1782. Having … the topic for my essay, I began working on it.
a) chose
b) chosen
c) choose
1783. She is considered the … portrait painter.
a) greeting

b) greatest
c) grander
1784. The detonator for a nuclear device may be made of … .
a) two equipment

b) two equipment pieces
c) two pieces of equipment
1785. An equilateral triangle is a triangle … .
a) that has three sides of equal length
b) it has three sides equally long
c) that have three sides of equal length
1786. Some students are confused … about these exams.
a) about
b) with
c) in
1787. … are found on the surface of the moon.
a) Craters and waterless seas that
b) Craters and waterless seas
c) Since craters and waterless seas
1788. Her … made her cry.
a) fearful
b) fearless
c) fearfulness
1789. … two waves pass a point simultaneously they will have no effect.
a) That
b) If
c) So that
1790. A child in the first grade tends to have … other children in the class.
a) the old like
b) the same as
c) the same age as
1791. I'm very … to succeed.
a) determine
b) determinant
c) determined

1792. This structure is so strong … difficult for anyone to penetrate it.
a) that it is
b) that is
c) and is
1793. I hoped … the game.
a) Brian to win
b) Brian's win
c) Brian would win

1794. This item is … that it's completely damaged.
a) oldest
b) so old
c) such an old

1795. Many Americans … a bowl of cereals every day.
a) are used to eating
b) used to eating
c) use to eat

1796. I will keep you safe … the crowd.
a) on
b) of
c) from

1797. The best form of treatment … mass inoculation.
a) it is
b) is
c) are

1798. I became bored … this work.
a) in
b) with
c) of

1799. We don't require that the students … a thesis in order to graduate.
a) write
b) will write
c) would write

1800. The oxygen of this planet is not … to support life.
a) too sufficient

b) sufficient
c) much sufficient

1801. He supported himself by … taxicabs.
a) driving
b) drive
c) to drive

1802. The kid viewed the … of a week alone without much enthusiasm.
a) prospective
b) prospector
c) prospects

1803. If you have a family history of heart disease you should make yearly appointments with … doctor.
a) his
b) your
c) yourself

1804. Support for research programs … much less than it was last year.
a) is
b) will
c) being

1805. Here, apartments cost more to rent than they … in other smaller cities.
a) did
b) will
c) do

1806. This model not only saves time but also … .
a) to save energy
b) saves energy
c) save energy

1807. The government requires that a census be taken every five years … accurate statistics may be compiled.
a) so that
b) such
c) such that

1808. The main … of economics success is out ability to forecast indicators.

a) determinant
b) determine
c) determined

1809. Who is responsible … the project?
a) to
b) with
c) for

1810. TV has little … for me.
a) attract
b) attraction
c) attractive

1811. The average life expectancy for people born during that year … 68
years.
a) have been
b) was
c) are

1812. A … mountaineer reached the top of the mountain last week.
a) fearless
b) fearful
c) fearfulness

1813. The flag is … in the morning and taken down at night.
a) risen
b) raised
c) raise

1814. One way to inform the public about this problem is through …
programs on TV.
a) industrial
b) agricultural
c) educational

1815. That book wasn't very … .
a) well written
b) well typed
c) good written

1816. These species can be divided into three groups, two of which …
extinct.

a) is
b) are
c) was

1817. Without alphabetical order dictionaries would be … to use.
a) possible
b) impossible
c) possibility

1818. I was shocked … the news of the accident.
a) from
b) being
c) with

1819. He was awarded the Nobel … for peace.
a) award
b) gift
c) prize

1820. The extent to which an individual is a product of either heredity or
environment … .
a) cannot be proved
b) cannot proved
c) cannot prove

1821. Every country … a national flag.
a) is
b) have
c) has

1822. Optical fibers … to deliver laser light.
a) can also use
b) can used
c) can also be used

1823. This project may or may not have been …
by her.
a) make
b) made
c) making

1824. Laptops for sale at … prices.
a) attractive

b) attraction
c) attractively

1825. Your mistakes are similar … his.
a) by
b) to
c) with

1826. A team of engineers is often … .
a) working on one project
b) no one project work
c) work on one project

1827. A vacuum will neither conduct hear nor
… .
a) sound waves are transmitted
b) transmitting sound waves
c) transmit sound waves

1828. To relieve pain cause by burns … .
a) take immediate steps

b) to take immediate steps
c) taking immediate steps
1829. All cereal grains … grow on the prairies
and plains of this country.
a) excepting rice
b) expect the rice
c) but rice
1830. They are freshmen , … whom come from
countryside.
a) most
b) most of
c) most of the
1831. … food is as nutritious for a baby as its
mother's milk.
a) No
b) Not
c) None
1832. Civil engineers had better … to use steel
supports in this structure.
a) plans
b) to plan
c) plan

1833. Several criminals escaped … prison
yesterday.
a) out
b) for
c) from
1834. The exam results could … your career.
a) determined
b) determine
c) determination
1835. If the oxygen supply … replenished by
plants, we would soon be
dead.
a) wasn't
b) weren't
c) hadn't been
1836. I used to earn … money.
a) many
b) lot
c) a lot of

1837. The legal implications of euthanasia are
so controversial … it is
illegal in most countries.
a) as
b) that
c) since
1838. Understanding lightning might help us …
life itself.
a) understand
b) understood
c) to understanding
1839. These species are particularly … because
of their unusual structures.
a) interest
b) interested
c) interesting
1840. … poetry is enjoyable when it is read
aloud.
a) Most
b) Almost
c) Many

1841. It is essential that cancer … diagnosed
early.
a) was
b) is
c) be
1842. Products in this shop are … arranged.
a) attract
b) attraction
c) attractively
1843. The battlefield was a … sight.
a) fearsome
b) fear
c) fearless
1844. This plant supports itself even when the
original supporting tree is …
longer alive.
a) not
b) no
c) any more
1845. Parents have great … for their children's
future.

a) expectant

b) expects

c) expectancies

1846. The consistency of this substance and that of glue … .

a) the same

b) are similar

c) they are alike

1847. The appliances in most homes use alternating current … .

a) instead direct current

b) for direct current instead

c) instead of direct current

1848. When Marry decided to run for another term, the opposition said she was … .

a) so old

b) too old

c) oldest

1849. This process results in an accumulation of … in porous rocks.

a) the oil

b) oil

c) oils

1850. We discussed the matter calmly and … .

a) reasonably

b) reason

c) reasoned

1851. I saw a sample … their work and it was impressing.

a) on

b) in

c) of

1852. It requires that two pieces of identification … .

a) presented

b) must present

c) be presented

Answer key:

1.a 2.a 3.c 4.c 5.b 6.c 7.c 8.a 9.c 10.b   11.c 12.c
13.a 14.b 15.c 16.c 17.a 18.c 19.b 20.c
21.a 22.c 23.b 24.c 25.a 26.c 27.a 28.b 29.c 30.a
31.c 32.a 33.b 34.b 35.c 36.a 37.a 38.c 39.c 40.b
41.a 42.c 43.b 44.a 45.c 46.c 47.c 48.b 49.a 50.b
51.b 52.c 53.b 54.a 55.c 56.b 57.b 58.c 59.c 60.a
61.b 62.c 63.a 64.b 65.c 66.c 67.a 68.b 69.c 70.a
71.b 72.b 73.c 74.b 75.a 76.a 77.c 78.c 79.b 80.a
81.c 82.c 83.a 84.b 85.c 86.c 87.b 88.a 89.b 90.c
91.b 92.a 93.c 94.b 95.c 96.b 97.a 98.c 99.b 100.a
101.c 102.c 103.a 104.b 105.c 106.c 107.a 108.b 109.a
110.c 111.b 112.c 113.c 114.a 115.b 116.c 117.a 118.b
119.c 120.a 121.b 122.a 123.c 124.b 125.c 126.b 127.a
128.c 129.c 130.a 131.b 132.c 133.a 134.a 135.c 136.b
137.a 138.b 139.c 140.c 141.c 142.a 143.b 144.c 145.c
146.a 147.a 148.b 149.c 150.b 151.a 152.c 153.c 154.b
155.c 156.a 157.b 158.b 159.c 160.a 161.b 162.c 163.c
164.b 165.a 166.b 167.c 168.a 169.b 170.c 171.c 172.b
173.b 174.c 175.a 176.b 177.a 178.c 179.a 180.b 181.a
182.c 183.b 184.c 185.b 186.c 187.a 188.a 189.c 190.b
191.a 192.c 193.c 194.b 195.c 196.a 197.c 198.b 199.a
200.c 201.b 202.a 203.c 204.b 205.c 206.a 207.c 208.b
209.a 210.c 211.c 212.a 213.b 214.a 215.c 216.b 217.c
218.b 219.b 220.b 221.a 222.c 223.c 224.b 225.c 226.a
227.b 228.c 229.b 230.a 231.c 232.b 233.c 234.a 235.c
236.b 237.c 238.c 239.b 240.a 241.b 242.a 243.c 244.b
245.b 246.b 247.a 248.c 249.b 250.a 251.b 252.c 253.c
254.c 255.a 256.c 257.b 258.c 259.c 260.c 261.b 262.a
263.c 264.a 265.b 266.c 267.a 268.c 269.a 270.b 271.b
272.a 273.b 274.c 275.c 276.a 277.b 278.a 279.c 280.b
281.c 282.c 283.c 284.a 285.c 286.b 287.c 288.b 289.c
290.a 291.a 292.b 293.c 294.c 295.c 296.a 297.b 298.a
299.b 300.a 301.a 302.c 303.c 304.b 305.b 306.b 307.c
308.b 309.a 310.c 311.c 312.c 313.a 314.b 315.c 316.b
317.c 318.a 319.c 320.c 321.a 322.b 323.c 324.c 325.b
326.a 327.c 328.b 329.a 330.c 331.c 332.c 333.a 334.b
335.b 336.a 337.b 338.c 339.a 340.c 341.b 342.a 343.c
344.b 345.b 346.c 347.c 348.b 349.a 350.c 351.b 352.a
353.c 354.a 355.c 356.b 357.b 358.a 359.c 360.b 361.c
362.a 363.c 364.b 365.a 366.c 367.c 368.a 369.b 370.c
371.b 372.a 373.c 374.a 375.b 376.c 377.c 378.a 379.a
380.c 381.a 382.c 383.b 384.b 385.c 386.c 387.a 388.b
389.c 390.c 391.b 392.c 393.a 394.c 395.a 396.c 397.b
398.c 399.a 400.b 401.a 402.b 403.b 404.c 405.c 406.b
407.a 408.a 409.c 410.a 411.c 412.a 413.b 414.b 415.c
416.a 417.c 418.b 419.c 420.a 421.b 422.a 423.c 424.b
425.b 426.a 427.c 428.b 429.b 430.a 431.c 432.c 433.b
434.c 435.c 436.b 437.a 438.c 439.c 440.a 441.b 442.c
443.a 444.b 445.c 446.c 447.b 448.a 449.c 450.b 451.b
452.a 453.c 454.a 455.b 456.c 457.c 458.a 459.c 460.b
461.c 462.b 463.c 464.a 465.c 466.b 467.b 468.c 469.c
470.a 471.a 472.c 473.b 474.b 475.c 476.a 477.b 478.a
479.c 480.b 481.c 482.a 483.b 484.c 485.b 486.c 487.b

119

488.c 489.a 490.a 491.b 492.c 493.a 494.b 495.a 496.c
497.a 498.c 499.b 500.a 501.a 502.b 503.c 504.a 505.b
506.c 507.a 508.c 509.b 510.a 511.c 512.b 513.a 514.c
515.a 516.c 517.b 518.a 519.b 520.c 521.a 522.c 523.b
524.a 525.c 526.a 527.b 528.a 529.c 530.c 531.b 532.a
533.c 534.b 535.a 536.b 537.b 538.a 539.c 540.a 541.c
542.a 543.c 544.b 545.b 546.c 547.c 548.a 549.c 550.b
551.b 552.b 553.a 554.c 555.c 556.c 557.b 558.b 559.a
560.b 561.c 562.b 563.c 564.a 565.b 566.c 567.b 568.c
569.c 570.a 571.b 572.c 573.b 574.a 575.a 576.c 577.b
578.b 579.c 580.b 581.c 582.a 583.b 584.b 585.a 586.c
587.b 588.c 589.b 590.c 591.b 592.c 593.a 594.b 595.a
596.a 597.c 598.b 599.c 600.a 601.b 602.a 603.c 604.a
605.a 606.c 607.b 608.a 609.c 610.b 611.c 612.c 613.a
614.b 615.a 616.c 617.b 618.c 619.a 620.b 621.c 622.b
623.a 624.b 625.b 626.b 627.a 628.c 629.c 630.a 631.b
632.a 633.c 634.c 635.b 636.b 637.c 638.a 639.a 640.c
641.c 642.a 643.c 644.b 645.b 646.a 647.b 648.b 649.c
650.a 651.b 652.a 653.c 654.c 655.a 656.a 657.b 658.c
659.b 660.c 661.c 662.a 663.c 664.c 665.a 666.b 667.c
668.b 669.a 670.c 671.b 672.a 673.c 674.c 675.a 676.b
677.c 678.c 679.b 680.a 681.a 682.c 683.b 684.b 685.c
686.b 687.c 688.b 689.c 690.c 691.a 692.c 693.b 694.c
695.a 696.b 697.c 698.b 699.c 700.b 701.a 702.c 703.c
704.b 705.a 706.b 707.a 708.b 709.c 710.b 711.b 712.c
713.a 714.c 715.a 716.c 717.a 718.c 719.c 720.b 721.a
722.c 723.b 724.a 725.c 726.c 727.b 728.a 729.c 730.b
731.a 732.b 733.a 734.c 735.b 736.c 737.b 738.a 739.c
740.b 741.b 742.c 743.a 744.b 745.a 746.c 747.b 748.a
749.c 750.b 751.a 752.b 753.c 754.c 755.a 756.b 757.a
758.c 759.c 760.a 761.a 762.c 763.c 764.b 765.b 766.c
767.b 768.c 769.a 770.b 771.b 772.a 773.c 774.b 775.c
776.a 777.c 778.b 779.a 780.c 781.c 782.b 783.a 784.c
785.b 786.c 787.c 788.c 789.a 790.b 791.c 792.b 793.c

794.b 795.c 796.b 797.a 798.b 799.a 800.c 801.b 802.b
803.a 804.c 805.a 806.c 807.b 808.c 809.c 810.b 811.a
812.c 813.b 814.a 815.b 816.a 817.c 818.a 819.b 820.a
821.b 822.b 823.c 824.c 825.a 826.b 827.c 828.a 829.a
830.b 831.a 832.c 833.b 834.a 835.a 836.c 837.b 838.c
839.b 840.b 841.c 842.c 843.a 844.b 845.b 846.a 847.c
848.c 849.b 850.a 851.a 852.b 853.c 854.b 855.c 856.a
857.c 858.c 859.b 860.a 861.c 862.a 863.c 864.c 865.b
866.b 867.c 868.c 869.a 870.b 871.a 872.b 873.b 874.c
875.a 876.b 877.c 878.b 879.c 880.a 881.c 882.b 883.a
884.c 885.b 886.c 887.b 888.a 889.b 890.b 891.b 892.a
893.c 894.c 895.a 896.b 897.c 898.b 899.a 900.c 901.b
902.a 903.c 904.a 905.a 906.c 907.b 908.b 909.c 910.b
911.c 912.a 913.b 914.c 915.a 916.c 917.c 918.a 919.c
920.c 921.c 922.a 923.c 924.b 925.a 926.c 927.b 928.a
929.b 930.c 931.a 932.b 933.c 934.b 935.a 936.a 937.c
938.c 939.b 940.a 941.c 942.c 943.a 944.b 945.b 946.c
947.a 948.b 949.c 950.b 951.a 952.c 953.b 954.c 955.a
956.c 957.a 958.a 959.a 960.b 961.c 962.c 963.b 964.c

965.a 966.c 967.b 968.b 969.c 970.a 971.b 972.c 973.a
974.b 975.c 976.a 977.b 978.a 979.b 980.c 981.c 982.a
983.b 984.b 985.c 986.a 987.b 988.c 989.a 990.b 991.c
992.c 993.b 994.c 995.a 996.c 997.b 998.c 999.a 1000.a
1001.b 1002.c 1003.a 1004.c 1005.b 1006.b 1007.a 1008.c
1009.a
1010.b 1011.b 1012.b 1013.a 1014.a 1015.a 1016.c 1017.b
1018.b
1019.a 1020.b 1021.a 1022.c 1023.a 1024.b 1025.c 1026.a
1027.c
1028.b 1029.b 1030.a 1031.a 1032.c 1033.a 1034.b 1035.b
1036.a
1037.c 1038.b 1039.a 1040.a 1041.b 1042.c 1043.b 1044.b
1045.a
1046.c 1047.b 1048.c 1049.a 1050.a 1051.b 1052.c 1053.b
1054.a
1055.c 1056.a 1057.b 1058.c 1059.b 1060.c 1061.b 1062.c
1063.b
1064.a 1065.b 1066.a 1067.c 1068.c 1069.c 1070.a 1071.a
1072.a
1073.b 1074.c 1075.b 1076.c 1077.b 1078.b 1079.b 1080.a
1081.b
1082.a 1083.c 1084.a 1085.b 1086.b 1087.a 1088.c 1089.b
1090.c
1091.b 1092.c 1093.a 1094.c 1095.a 1096.b 1097.c 1098.b
1099.b
1100.a 1101.b 1102.c 1103.a 1104.b 1105.c 1106.c 1107.a
1108.b
1109.a 1110.c 1111.a 1112.c 1113.b 1114.a 1115.b 1116.c
1117.a
1118.a 1119.b 1120.c 1121.c 1122.a 1123.b 1124.a 1125.a
1126.c
1127.b 1128.a 1129.b 1130.c 1131.a 1132.b 1133.c 1134.b
1135.c

1136.b 1137.b 1138.c 1139.a 1140.b 1141.c 1142.a 1143.b
1144.a
1145.c 1146.b 1147.b 1148.a 1149.c 1150.b 1151.b 1152.a
1153.c
1154.c 1155.a 1156.b 1157.c 1158.a 1159.c 1160.c 1161.b
1162.b
1163.c 1164.a 1165.a 1166.b 1167.c 1168.a 1169.a 1170.b
1171.b
1172.a 1173.b 1174.c 1175.a 1176.a 1177.b 1178.c 1179.b
1180.b
1181.b 1182.a 1183.c 1184.c 1185.c 1186.c 1187.a 1188.b
1189.b
1190.c 1191.a 1192.c 1193.b 1194.c 1195.c 1196.a 1197.a
1198.b
1199.c 1200.b 1201.a 1202.c 1203.b 1204.c 1205.c 1206.b
1207.a
1208.c 1209.c 1210.b 1211.b 1212.a 1213.c 1214.a 1215.c
1216.a

1217.a 1218.b 1219.b 1220.c 1221.b 1222.b 1223.a 1224.c 1225.b

1226.a 1227.c 1228.c 1229.c 1230.a 1231.b 1232.c 1233.a 1234.a

1235.c 1236.b 1237.c 1238.b 1239.a 1240.c 1241.a 1242.b 1243.c

1244.b 1245.c 1246.a 1247.b 1248.a 1249.c 1250.c 1251.a 1252.c

1253.b 1254.a 1255.c 1256.c 1257.a 1258.c 1259.b 1260.c 1261.a

1262.c 1263.b 1264.a 1265.c 1266.a 1267.a 1268.c 1269.b 1270.a

1271.a 1272.c 1273.b 1274.a 1275.c 1276.b 1277.c 1278.b 1279.a

1280.b 1281.b 1282.c 1283.a 1284.c 1285.c 1286.b 1287.a 1288.a

1289.b 1290.c 1291.a 1292.b 1293.c 1294.a 1295.c 1296.b 1297.b

1298.a 1299.b 1300.c 1301.c 1302.a 1303.b 1304.a 1305.c 1306.c

1307.a 1308.b 1309.c 1310.c 1311.a 1312.c 1313.b 1314.c 1315.a

1316.a 1317.c 1318.c 1319.b 1320.b 1321.b 1322.c 1323.a 1324.b

1325.c 1326.b 1327.c 1328.a 1329.b 1330.b 1331.a 1332.c 1333.a

1334.b 1335.c 1336.b 1337.a 1338.b 1339.a 1340.c 1341.a 1342.b

1343.c 1344.c 1345.a 1346.c 1347.b 1348.b 1349.a 1350.c 1351.a

1352.c 1353.b 1354.c 1355.a 1356.c 1357.b 1358.c 1359.c 1360.a

1361.c 1362.b 1363.a 1364.c 1365.a 1366.b 1367.c 1368.a 1369.c

1370.b 1371.c 1372.c 1373.a 1374.b 1375.c 1376.a 1377.c 1378.b

1379.a 1380.c 1381.b 1382.c 1383.b 1384.a 1385.b 1386.c 1387.c

1388.c 1389.a 1390.b 1391.c 1392.a 1393.c 1394.a 1395.c 1396.a

1397.a 1398.c 1399.b 1400.c 1401.b 1402.a 1403.c 1404.b 1405.a

1406.c 1407.c 1408.b 1409.a 1410.c 1411.b 1412.a 1413.c 1414.c

1415.a 1416.b 1417.a 1418.b 1419.a 1420.c 1421.c 1422.a 1423.b

1424.b 1425.c 1426.a 1427.b 1428.c 1429.b 1430.b 1431.a 1432.c

1433.b 1434.c 1435.b 1436.c 1437.a 1438.c 1439.c 1440.b 1441.b

1442.a 1443.c 1444.b 1445.a 1446.a 1447.c 1448.b 1449.a 1450.c

1451.b 1452.a 1453.a 1454.b 1455.c 1456.a 1457.c 1458.b 1459.c

1460.b 1461.b 1462.a 1463.c 1464.c 1465.b 1466.c 1467.b 1468.c

1469.a 1470.b 1471.a 1472.c 1473.c 1474.b 1475.b 1476.a 1477.b

1478.c 1479.a 1480.c 1481.a 1482.b 1483.c 1484.b 1485.a 1486.b

1487.c 1488.a 1489.c 1490.b 1491.a 1492.c 1493.b 1494.a 1495.c

1496.a 1497.b 1498.b 1499.c 1500.a 1501.b 1502.c 1503.a 1504.a

1505.b 1506.a 1507.c 1508.b 1509.b 1510.a 1511.a 1512.b 1513.c

1514.c 1515.a 1516.c 1517.a 1518.b 1519.c 1520.a 1521.b 1522.a

1523.c 1524.a 1525.c 1526.b 1527.b 1528.a 1529.c 1530.b 1531.c

1532.b 1533.c 1534.a 1535.c 1536.b 1537.a 1538.c 1539.b 1540.a

1541.a 1542.c 1543.b 1544.a 1545.b 1546.c 1547.a 1548.b 1549.c

1550.a 1551.b 1552.a 1553.c 1554.b 1555.c 1556.b 1557.c 1558.a

1559.b 1560.c 1561.a 1562.c 1563.b 1564.a 1565.c 1566.c 1567.b

1568.b 1569.a 1570.c 1571.c 1572.b 1573.a 1574.b 1575.b 1576.c

1577.c 1578.b 1579.c 1580.c 1581.b 1582.a 1583.c 1584.b 1585.a

1586.c 1587.a 1588.b 1589.a 1590.c 1591.b 1592.c 1593.c 1594.a

1595.a 1596.c 1597.b 1598.c 1599.a 1600.b 1601.c 1602.c 1603.a

1604.b 1605.b 1606.c 1607.b 1608.c 1609.c 1610.a 1611.b 1612.b

1613.a 1614.c 1615.b 1616.a 1617.b 1618.a 1619.c 1620.c 1621.b

1622.a 1623.c 1624.a 1625.b 1626.a 1627.c 1628.b 1629.a 1630.b

1631.a 1632.c 1633.b 1634.c 1635.a 1636.c 1637.a 1638.c 1639.b

1640.c 1641.a 1642.c 1643.b 1644.c 1645.c 1646.a 1647.c 1648.a

1649.b 1650.a 1651.a 1652.b 1653.c 1654.a 1655.c 1656.b 1657.c

1658.a 1659.c 1660.b 1661.a 1662.c 1663.c 1664.b 1665.b 1666.b

1667.a 1668.b 1669.c 1670.c 1671.a 1672.c 1673.b 1674.a 1675.c

1676.a 1677.b 1678.c 1679.a 1680.c 1681.a 1682.c 1683.a 1684.b

1685.b 1686.c 1687.c 1688.c 1689.b 1690.a 1691.a 1692.b 1693.a

1694.c 1695.a 1696.b 1697.b 1698.c 1699.c 1700.c 1701.b
1702.a
1703.c 1704.a 1705.b 1706.a 1707.c 1708.c 1709.b 1710.a
1711.c
1712.c 1713.a 1714.b 1715.a 1716.c 1717.b 1718.b 1719.c
1720.a
1721.c 1722.b 1723.c 1724.a 1725.c 1726.a 1727.b 1728.b
1729.b
1730.c 1731.c 1732.a 1733.b 1734.b 1735.a 1736.c 1737.a
1738.a
1739.c 1740.b 1741.c 1742.c 1743.b 1744.a 1745.b 1746.a
1747.c
1748.a 1749.c 1750.c 1751.b 1752.c 1753.b 1754.c 1755.c
1756.a
1757.b 1758.a 1759.c 1760.b 1761.a 1762.b 1763.c 1764.b
1765.a
1766.a 1767.c 1768.a 1769.b 1770.a 1771.c 1772.a 1773.b
1774.a
1775.c 1776.a 1777.a 1778.b 1779.c 1780.b 1781.a 1782.b
1783.b
1784.c 1785.a 1786.a 1787.b 1788.c 1789.b 1790.c 1791.c
1792.a
1793.c 1794.b 1795.a 1796.c 1797.b 1798.b 1799.a 1800.b
1801.a
1802.c 1803.b 1804.a 1805.c 1806.b 1807.a 1808.a 1809.c
1810.b
1811.b 1812.a 1813.b 1814.c 1815.a 1816.b 1817.b 1818.c
1819.c

1820.a 1821.c 1822.c 1823.b 1824.a 1825.b 1826.a 1827.c
1828.a
1829.c 1830.b 1831.a 1832.c 1833.c 1834.b 1835.b 1836.c
1837.b
1838.a 1839.c 1840.a 1841.c 1842.c 1843.a 1844.b 1845.c
1846.b
1847.c 1848.b 1849.b 1850.a 1851.c 1852.c